STEP

C000203644

Usin
Amstrad
PCW9512

Using the Amstrad PCW 9512

John Campbell

HEINEMANN
NEW TECH

Heinemann Newtech
An imprint of Heinemann Professional Publishing Ltd
Halley Court, Jordan Hill, Oxford OX2 8EJ

OXFORD   LONDON   MELBOURNE   AUCKLAND   SINGAPORE
IBADAN   NAIROBI   GABORONE   KINGSTON

First published 1988
Reprinted 1989 (twice)

British Library Cataloguing in Publication Data
Campbell, J. (John)
Using the Amstrad PCW9512
1. Amstrad PCW9512 microcomputer systems
I. Title
004.165

ISBN 0 434 90201 2

Typeset by JCA, Ringwood, Hampshire
Printed and bound in Great Britain
by Redwood Burn Limited, Trowbridge, Wiltshire

Contents

Contents

What I have done in this book is to examine the Amstrad PCW9512 through the eyes of someone who doesn't know (or want to know) the first thing about what goes on under the bonnet of a computer — the sort of person (like me) who will be using the machine mainly for doing normal word-processing work.

I have concentrated on those day-to-day activities that we carry out on a routine basis when we are preparing text. Consequently the book has six parts — each one dealing with a different kind of activity. Each part contains a number of Sections containing step-by-step explanations of how to do the sort of jobs you will want to do with the PCW.

I don't expect that anyone will want to read this book from cover to cover like a novel (the story-line is a bit thin for that, though the plot is quite detailed). It has been designed as a source of quick reference for those moments when your mind goes blank and you can't remember what to do next.

Each Section is, as far as possible, self-contained. However, to avoid endless repetition of information — such as how to get to the Disk Management Screen — a certain amount of detail from Part 1 is assumed in the later Sections.

Throughout the text, the keys that you should press are always printed in square brackets and in bold type, e.g. **[SPACEBAR]** or **[SHIFT]** or **[EXIT]** or **[ENTER]** or the letter **[C]**.

Each of the steps in a procedure for effecting some action or other is indicated by a large bold number and gives the keys that should be pressed and tells you how the PCW should respond.

Interspersed among the steps are notes providing background information and facts you need if you are to understand why certain things have to be done in certain ways. A Glossary is also provided at the back of this book should you temporarily have forgotten what something means.

PART ONE

Basic skills

■ SECTION 1
Introduction

You can use your PCW simply as a **word processor** or you can use it as a **general-purpose computer**. You can even, if you wish, use it as an **electronic typewriter**:

■ To use it as a word processor, controlled by the Locoscript 2 software programs, you will need a copy of the disk labelled **Locoscript 2**.

■ To use it as a general-purpose computer, running many different kinds of software package (including other word processing software), you will need a copy of the disk labelled **CP/M Plus**.

■ To use it as an electronic typewriter, follow the instructions given in Section 6.

IMPORTANT NOTE   When you start up for the first time you will almost certainly be obliged to use the original Locoscript 2 and CP/M Plus disks supplied with your machine. However, once you have the machine running you should make duplicate copies of these disks as described in Section 4. The originals should then be stored safely and only the copies used when starting up. Then, should you inadvertently damage the copies in any way, you will have the originals to take further working copies from.

■ SECTION 2
Start-up for word processing

1 Plug the machine in to the mains. Turn the mains switch on and then turn the machine on with the push-button at the rear of the monitor.

2 Take the disk labelled **Locoscript 2** out of its clear plastic case and put it in the disk drive slot (the left-hand one if you have two drive slots). Make sure that side 1 of the disk is uppermost.

3 After a few moments you should see the light on the drive glow and you should hear the disk drive whirring. If nothing seems to happen for some time, try tapping the long **[SPACEBAR]** on the keyboard just once.

4 You should see a pattern of horizontal lines start to appear on your screen. If the screen flashes, or if the PCW beeps at you in a plaintive way, you have put the wrong disk in the drive — or perhaps the right disk but upside down. Put the correct disk in (with side 1 uppermost) and tap the [SPACEBAR].

5 You will have to wait for a few moments while the PCW "reads" the Locoscript software and loads a copy of it into its memory (the original is still on the disk and is not changed at all).

You will know when the software is loaded because the screen will display a pattern of boxes and columns with names in them. The top three lines will be displayed in reverse video (black on white rather than white on black like the rest of the screen). This is Locoscript's **Disk Management Screen**, which seems very intimidating at first, but read on...

Start-up for word processing

```
                    Disc management.                  Printer idle. Using none.
C=Create new document       E=Edit document      P=Print document     D=Direct printing
f1=Actions  f2=Disc  f3=File  f4=Group  f5=Document  f6=Settings  f7=Disc change  f8=Options
```

```
Drive A:                   Drive B:      not fitted  Drive M:
173k used   0k free  12 files   0k used  0k free  0 files   2k used  60k free   2 files

group 0 173k   group 4  0k                          group 0  2k   group 4  0k
group 1   0k   group 5  0k                          group 1  0k   group 5  0k
group 2   0k   group 6  0k                          group 2  0k   group 6  0k
group 3   0k   group 7  0k                          group 3  0k   group 7  0k
```

```
A: group 0   12 files  M: group 0    2 files
   0 limbo files          0 limbo files

LOCOCHAR.2    65k         2 hidden    2k
LOCOCHAR.3     8k
LOCOCHAR.BAS  14k
LOCOCHAR.KEY   1k
PHRASES .STD   1k
READ    .ME    6k
SETTINGS.STD   1k
   5 hidden  117k
```

All but the top three lines of the screen are taken up by details about the disk drives you have available – this is simply for information purposes and needn't worry you just yet.

The top three lines (in reverse video) are concerned with Locoscript itself and will stay on screen at all times when you are using Locoscript, though the information on them will change to reflect what you are doing at the time. The top line reminds you what you are doing, the other two lines provide a list of tasks that you can carry out from this point in the program.

```
                    Disc management.                  Printer idle. Using none.
C=Create new document       E=Edit document      P=Print document     D=Direct printing
f1=Actions  f2=Disc  f3=File  f4=Group  f5=Document  f6=Settings  f7=Disc change  f8=Options
```

Note It is as if you have walked into a building via the main doors and you found yourself in a hallway with lots of doors leading off – each one labelled with a different task (C to Create a new document, E to Edit an existing document and so on). You can take any one of those doors now, but you must come back to the hallway before you can go through another doorway to do a

■ SECTION 2
Start-up for word processing

different task or leave Locoscript via the main doors again. If you don't leave via the main doors, you may destroy the work you have done. So this Disk Management Screen is very important to you, when you start up, when you change tasks *AND* when you close down.

The screen display just below the three bright lines gives you information about three disk drives. **Drive A** is the one that holds the Locoscript disk (the left-hand slot if you have two); **drive B** is the second drive on a twin drive machine (the right-hand slot); and **drive M** is the **memory drive**. Drive M is very easy to use and it responds far more quickly than either A or B, *but beware!* As its name implies, drive M is not really a disk drive — it is simply a part of the PCW's memory that has been set aside to work as if it were a disk drive!

Drive A:				Drive B:	not fitted		Drive M:			
173k used	0k free	12 files		0k used	0k free	0 files	2k used	60k free	2 files	
group 0 173K	group 4	0k					group 0	2k	group 4	0k
group 1	0k	group 5	0k				group 1	0k	group 5	0k
group 2	0k	group 6	0k				group 2	0k	group 6	0k
group 3	0k	group 7	0k				group 3	0k	group 7	0k

When you switch the PCW off, its memory is emptied and you lose whatever was in it. So think of the memory drive as a temporary lodging place for your work.

Closing down

1 When you are ready to close down, get back to the Disk Management screen (Locoscript will tell you how).

2 If you have been working on the memory drive (drive M) make sure you have a permanent copy of all the documents you want to keep (by copying the document files onto a disk — see Section 10).

3 When you have finished and you are satisfied that you have safety copies of everything you need, remove the disk(s) and switch off the machine.

Note It is good practice to check that the drive slots are empty *before* switching the PCW on or off.

■ SECTION 3

Start-up for general computing

1 Plug the machine into the mains. Turn the mains switch on and then turn the machine on with the push-button at the rear of the monitor.

2 Take the disk labelled **CP/M Plus** out of its clear plastic case and put it in the disk drive slot (the left-hand one if you have two drive slots). Make sure that side 1 of the disk is uppermost.

3 After a few moments you should see the light on the drive glow and you should hear the disk drive whirring. If nothing seems to happen for some time, try tapping the long **[SPACEBAR]** on the keyboard just once.

4 You should see a pattern of horizontal lines start to appear on your screen. If the screen flashes, or if the PCW beeps at you in a plaintive way, you have put the wrong disk in the drive — or perhaps the right disk, but upside down. Put the correct disk in (with side 1 uppermost) and tap the **[SPACEBAR]**.

5 You will see various messages appear on the screen as the PCW automatically carries out several tasks. After a short while you will see the display settle down and you will get CP/M's **system prompt** — **A**> — which is sometimes called the **A prompt**.

```
CP/M Plus  Amstrad Consumer Electronics plc
v 1.4, 61K TPA, 1 disc drive, 112K drive M:
A)█
```

You are now ready to key in commands to operate the PCW as a computer. Provided that you have the appropriate software programs available you can carry out any housekeeping task you like, or you can run all sorts of software programs.

■ SECTION 4
Making a duplicate copy of a disk

Although this section deals with making duplicate copies of disks in general, the first disks that you duplicate should be your **Locoscript** and **CP/M Plus** disks. You will then have working copies to use in your future work and the originals can be stored safely away — to await the day when you find that somehow your working copies have been damaged. You can then go back to the originals and take a fresh set of working copies!

So, the first time you carry out the following procedure you will have to read 'original disk' for 'working copy of the disk'.

Resetting/booting your system

1 Start by putting your working copy of the CP/M Plus disk in the disk drive (the left-hand one if you have two disk drive slots). Make sure side 1 is uppermost.

2 With your left hand, hold down the keys labelled **[SHIFT]** and **[EXTRA]**. Then, with your right hand, tap the key labelled **[EXIT]**.

You will see the PCW go through its CP/M start-up sequence. This procedure is known as **re-setting** or **booting** your system.

When you reset with the CP/M Plus disk in the drive and you have the **A>** prompt on screen, CP/M is ready to accept your commands.

Copying: the DISCKIT program

You want to copy a disk and to do that you need to use a program called **DISCKIT** which is on your CP/M Plus disk (which should still be in drive A). Don't forget, too, to have a new or blank disk handy! Then:

1 Key in **DISCKIT** and press **[RETURN]**. The PCW responds by running the DISCKIT program. You'll see a message on screen telling you how many disk drives DISCKIT has found, asking you to remove the disk(s) and then press a key.

2 Push the button on the front of the disk drive to release the disk and then tap the **[SPACEBAR]**.

■ SECTION 4
Making a duplicate copy of a disk

3 DISCKIT displays a **menu** that offers you four options.

> **COPY** (tap the key labelled **f6/f5**)
> **FORMAT** (tap **f4/f3**)
> **VERIFY** (tap **f2/f1**)
> **EXIT** (tap the **[EXIT]** key to leave **DISCKIT**)

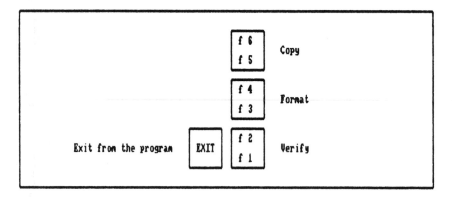

4 We want to copy a disk, so tap the **[f6/f5]** key (which can be found in the pad of keys at the left of the keyboard).

How you continue now depends on whether you have a single drive or twin drive machine.

Copying: single drive machines

1 DISCKIT asks you to put the disk you want to read – copy *from* – in the drive and then tap the letter **[Y]**.

2 Put the disk you want to copy from into the drive, then tap **[Y]**. Have your new or blank disk ready.

Copying: twin drive machines

DISCKIT asks you which drive you want to read – copy *from*. Tap **f4/f3** for drive A or **f2/f1** for drive B.

■ SECTION 4
Making a duplicate copy of a disk

3   Put the disk you want to copy (*from*) in drive A, and then tap **[f4/f3]**. Put the disk on which you want the copy (the one you want to copy *to*) in drive B and tap **[f2/f1]**. Then tap the letter **[Y]**.

Completing the copy

DISCKIT will now copy your disk for you. If you have a single drive machine (or if you have elected to read from one drive and write to the same one) DISCKIT will prompt you to swap disks at the appropriate times.

If the disk you are writing to is brand new you will see a message telling you that DISCKIT will **FORMAT** while it is copying (see Section 5).

While copying bear in mind the following:

■ Get into the habit of always putting the disk in a drive with side 1 uppermost.

■ If, during the copy process, you are asked to swap disks and you put the wrong disk in the drive, or put the right disk in upside down, DISCKIT will spot your mistake and ask you to rectify it.

■ If, during the copy process, you do not push the disk home securely in the drive, DISCKIT will think that the disk is missing altogether and it will prompt you to provide the right disk and then tap **[R]** to retry the activity (or **[C]** to cancel).

Complete the procedure as follows:

1   When prompted by DISCKIT, remove the disk(s) and tap the **[SPACEBAR]**. DISCKIT will ask if you want to make another copy.

2   If yes, tap the **[Y]** key and repeat the process.

3   If no, tap the **[SPACEBAR]**. DISCKIT will display its main menu again (the one with four options).

Making a duplicate copy of a disk

4   Tap **[EXIT]** to leave DISCKIT.

5   Label your newly copied disk!

Remember that it is a good idea to keep programs and data on separate disks. If nothing else, you will be able to get more data on a disk if it is dedicated to the job!

■ SECTION 5
Formatting a new disk

Before you can use a new disk to hold data files (or program files for that matter) you will have to go through a procedure to prepare the disk for its job. When you get a brand new disk it is simply a thin sheet of plastic material coated with a magnetic medium. Before you can use it to store information of any kind, you will have to 'mark out' a pattern of tracks on the surface. These tracks hold the magnetic 'pigeon-holes' for the data and they have to be laid out in a very precise format. That is why the preparation procedure is known as **formatting** the disk.

Formatting is very easy to do — dangerously easy! *So follow this procedure exactly!*

1 Have your CP/M disk to hand as well as your brand new disk or disks.

2 Start by putting the working copy of the CP/M Plus disk in the disk drive (the left-hand one if you have two disk drive slots). Make sure side 1 is uppermost.

3 With your left hand, hold down the keys labelled **[SHIFT]** and **[EXTRA]**. Then, with your right hand, tap the key labelled **[EXIT]**.

You will see the PCW go through its CP/M start-up sequence. This procedure is known as **resetting** or **booting** your system. When you reset with the CP/M Plus disk in the drive and you have the **A>** prompt on screen, CP/M is ready to accept your command.

You want to format a disk and to do that you need to use a program called **DISCKIT** which is on your CP/M Plus disk (which should still be in drive A), so continue with the procedure as follows:

4 Key in **DISCKIT** and press **[RETURN]**. The PCW responds by running the DISCKIT program. You'll see a message on screen telling you how many disk drives DISCKIT has found, asking you to remove the disk(s) and then press a key.

5 Push the button on the front of the disk drive to release the disk and then tap the **[SPACEBAR]**.

■ SECTION 5
Formatting a new disk

6 DISCKIT will display a **menu** that offers you four options:

COPY (tap the key labelled **f6/f5**)
FORMAT (tap **f4/f3**)
VERIFY (tap **f2/f1**)
EXIT (tap **[EXIT]** key to leave DISCKIT)

7 You want to format a disk, so tap the **[f4/f3]** key (which can be found in the pad of keys at the left of the keyboard). On a single drive machine you will be asked to provide the disk to be formatted. On a twin drive machine you will be asked to tell DISCKIT which drive will hold the disk to be formatted (I recommend that you get into the habit of putting the disk in drive B — with side 1 uppermost — and then nominating that drive).

8 When you are sure that you are ready, tap **[Y]** to start the formatting process. You will see DISCKIT keep a count as it lays down 160 tracks (numbered 0 to 159) on the surface of the disk.

BEWARE! **You can use the FORMATTING process on any disk.** Make sure before you start that the disk you intend to FORMAT is really one that you can wipe clean without losing some vital information. Especially guard against formatting any program disks!

■ SECTION 6
Using the PCW as an electronic typewriter

1 Switch your machine on and start up with the working copy of your Locoscript 2 disk. Wait until the PCW displays the Disk Management Screen.

2 If you look in the middle of the three bright lines at the top, towards the right-hand end you will see **D=Direct printing**.

3 Tap the letter **[D]**.

Note The PCW does not keep a copy of the text you key in while you are using the PCW as an electronic typewriter. If you want to keep copies of your work use the **[C]** option to Create a new document, or the **[E]** option to Edit an existing one.

4 You will see a small **FLAG MENU** appear near the top of the screen, in the middle. Tap the **[ENTER]** key. The screen clears and then presents you with a display which looks like a blank page (see Section 8).

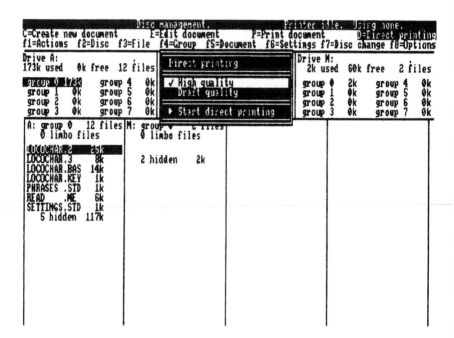

5 As you are about to do some direct printing (or, to put it in the jargon, you are now in **direct printing mode**), check your printer.

6 First, check that the printer's **tractor feed** (for continuous stationery) is *not* fitted. (If it is fitted, remove it by unclipping the front edge and then lift and hinge the unit backward, so the two hooks at the back of the unit clear their locating holes.) Fit the **paper tray**.

7 Take a sheet of your typing paper and slip it gently between the casing of the printer and the back surface of the printer **platen** (the black rubber roller). Line up the left-hand edge of the paper with the second rib on the printer casing.

Towards the right-hand end of the platen you will see two levers. The one to the rear of the platen is the **paper release lever**, the one just in front of the platen is the **paper load lever**.

8 Move the paper *load* lever towards the front of the printer to its *fullest* extent. This lever has two positions and you should move it through the first 'stop' to the second. Then let it return about a third of the way back to the first 'stop'. The printer will now feed your paper in, leaving it in position ready for you to start printing.

9 If you want to adjust the position of the paper, move the paper *release* lever toward the front of the printer. This will allow you to move the paper into the right position.

10 When you have finished adjusting your paper, reset the paper release lever *and* the paper load lever.

When you load the printer with this procedure the PCW assumes that you may want to make a number of adjustments to the printer, so it automatically goes into its **printer control state** (or MODE). If you look at the three bright lines at the top of the screen you will see that they have changed (notice particularly that **PCW9512** is flashing at the left of the second line).

11 If you want to make adjustments to any of the printer settings, now is the time to do it. For our purposes now, just tap the **[EXIT]** key to escape from the printer control state. The normal blank page screen should reappear.

12 You are now ready to key in your text (see Section 9).

Note the following:

■ Nothing will appear on the printer until you press the **[RETURN]** key.

■ Don't worry about fitting words onto lines, just concentrate on keying in the text and let the PCW fit your text onto the page line by line. If you hit the wrong letter while you are typing, just tap ←**[DEL]** to delete the letter and then key it in again.

■ When you have finished typing your text, check and amend your work *before* you press **[RETURN]** (see Sections 12 and 13). If you want to leave blank lines(s) in your text, tap the **[RETURN]** key once for each line to be left blank.

Continue as follows:

13 Key in some text (your name will do for now), check it and then press **[RETURN]**. Notice how the screen clears as the printer prints your text.

14 Tap the **[RETURN]** key a couple of times to leave two blank lines and then key in enough text to fill up three or four lines on the screen.

15 Tap the **[RETURN]** key to print your text. Then tap the **[EXIT]** key.

You will see another **flag menu** appear on the screen. This is a typical example of how the Locoscript software prompts you to tell it what to do next. Here you are offered two options. If you choose the first one, the printer will finish printing your text

23

before **exiting** from direct printing mode. The second one stops immediately and you lose your text. To select the option you want, move the highlighted bar on the menu with the **cursor control keys**, the four keys marked with arrows in the pad at the far right of the keyboard. Alternatively, you can simply key in the initial letter of the one you want. Once you have the bar over the option you want, tap the **[ENTER]** key to 'enter' your selection into the PCW's memory.

16 For our purposes, just tap the **[ENTER]** key now. The PCW displays the Disk Management Screen again, ready for you to select your next task.

■ SECTION 7
About the disk drives

The **Disk Management Screen** (obtained as described in Section 2) displays two main types of information:

■ The top three lines (in reverse video, i.e. black letters on white rather than white letters on black) are to do with the way Locoscript works.

■ The rest of the screen gives you information about the disk drives on your machine.

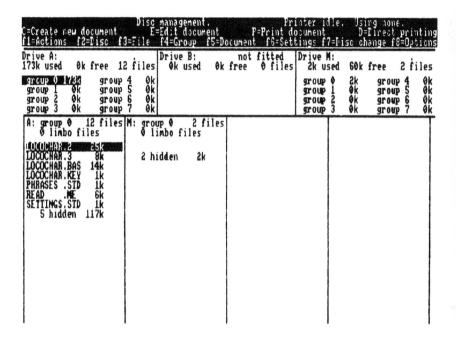

The information about your disk drives is in turn broken into two types:

■ The oblong boxes, just below the Locoscript information, tell you about the disk drives themselves.

■ The columns of information which take up the rest of the screen, are the names of **files** held on the disk drives.
Every PCW has *at least* two drives, A and M:

■ **Drive A** This is the physical disk drive – the slot – on the *front left* of the main unit. (If you have another drive slot on the *front right* of the unit, this is drive B.)

■ **Drive M** This is not actually a disk drive − it is a part of the PCW's **memory** that has been set aside to respond *as if it were* a disk drive.

Because it is electronic rather than mechanical, the **memory drive** (drive M) works much faster than an actual disk drive − which is the main advantage of having it. **But beware** − when you switch the PCW off you lose everything in its memory circuits − including the memory drive! So, if you want to keep a copy of your work you *must* put that copy on one of your disks before you switch off.

Moving the bright bars

When you **create** a new document file, you have to start by deciding where on your disks you intend to keep that file while you are working on it. When you want to **edit** a file that already exists, start by selecting the file you want to work with. You do both these jobs by moving the bright bars on the screen. So how do you do that?

1 Find the **cursor control keys** − the four keys marked with arrows in the pad of keys at the right-hand end of your keyboard. Tap the ↓ key just once. The bright bar in the first column moves down one line to highlight the second filename in the list. But notice that the bright bar in the first oblong box has not moved.

2 Now hold down a **[SHIFT]** key and tap ↓ *twice.*

This time the bright bar in the first oblong box does move down and at the same time the bright bar in the columns area moves two columns to the right. Why is that? The upper of the bright bars highlights the name of a **group** of files, while the lower bright bar highlights the name of a file **within the highlighted group**. (If you look at the name at the top of the column you will see that it is the same as the name being highlighted in the oblong box.)

26

About the disk drives

The **upper** bright bar is your **groups cursor**. The **lower** bright bar is your **files cursor**.

Note The groups cursor is still in the box headed Drive A, but also notice that there is a box for Drive B (whether you have one fitted or not) and there is a box for Drive M.

3 Hold down a [SHIFT] key, keep an eye on the screen and tap → twice (four times if you have twin drives). Your groups cursor moves to drive M.

4 Hold down a [SHIFT] key and tap ↑ once, then tap ← twice (four times if you have twin drives) and release the [SHIFT] key. When the screen settles down again, tap ↓ (*unshifted*) and move the files cursor onto the file called **DISCINFO**.

5 Now tap [E] as if you were going to EDIT a file. A flag menu appears, asking you to confirm that you do want to edit a file named DISCINFO which is in group 1 on drive A.

6 That *is* what we want to do so tap the [ENTER] key to confirm. Nothing seems to happen for a second or so, but then the PCW displays the file contents on the screen. So that is how you select a file when you want to EDIT it (or perhaps just read it).

■ SECTION 7
About the disk drives

```
A: group 1/DISCINFJ.      Editing text.              Printer idle.  Using A: M:
Main:      Pil0    LS1    CR+0   LP6                        Page  1  line  1/54
f1=Actions    f2=Layout    f3=Style    f4=Size    f5=Page    f7=Spall    f8=Options    EXIT
```

Keeping your discs organised↵
↵
It is very easy to create document after document with no clear
scheme suggesting the disk you store them on, the groups you
keep them in or the names you give your documents. The result
is rather like stuffing sheets of paper into drawers. While you
don't have many sheets of paper, it is quite possible to find
the one you want, but the moment your drawers start to get
full, it is a hopeless task finding anything.↵
↵
The solution with the drawers is to tidy them up, grouping
together some sheets of paper and moving others to a different
drawer. Similarly, the solution to your problem with discs is
also to tidy them up. You can work a lot more efficiently:↵
↵
- if you use different disks for different types of documents,
rather like you would use the different drawers of a filing
cabinet↵
↵
- if you use the different groups on a disk like you would use
different folders within the filing cabinet↵
↵
- if you give your disks, groups and documents names that help
you remember what information they contain.↵
↵
In this session, we shall discuss:↵
↵
- how to get new discs ready for use↵

7 Tap the [EXIT] key, and then [A] to highlight the **Abandon edit** option on the flag menu. Now tap the [ENTER] key to tell the PCW to go ahead.

Creating a new document file

When you want to create a brand new document file the procedure is similar except, of course, there will be no file name for you to highlight. So all you have to do is move your cursor to the group you want to use to store the file and then tap [C] like this:

1 Move the groups cursor down one line ([SHIFT] and ↓) so the file cursor lands on a file called **TEMPLATE.STD** in the letters group column. Now [C].

About the disk drives

2   When you see the flag menu, just tap **[ENTER]**. The PCW presents you with a blank 'page', but you can see that it is not completely blank. In fact it is set up ready to lay out your work in the form of a letter (see Section 8).

3   For now, just tap **[EXIT]**, then **[A]**, then **[ENTER]** to get back to the Disk Management Screen.

■ SECTION 8

Interpreting the Page display

1 Switch on and go to the Disk Management Screen (see Section 2).

2 To get the Page display on screen we will select the **[E]** option from this screen. With this option you must begin by moving your group and file cursors to the name of the file you want to edit.

3 Tap → to get to 'Group 1' on disk A. Tap repeatedly until the file cursor ends up on the file called **TABS.EG**, then tap **[E]**. A flag menu appears. This one is asking you to confirm that you want to edit the document which is described by the details on the menu.

4 If the details are as I specified, tap the **[Enter]** key to tell the PCW to go ahead.

After a slight pause the Disk Management Screen clears and is replaced with the Page display. Ignore the text for the moment. Note:

■ The three bright lines at the top of the screen (the **Locoscript control area**) are still there, but the information on those lines has changed.

■ Just below the Locoscript control area there is a row of dots which has some small numbers and three right-facing arrows just above it. You will see that the row of dots extends right across the screen. At every tenth dot there is a number, so the position of the number 4 tells you where the 40th character will appear *on the screen.*

Interpreting the Page display

```
A: group 1/1989    EG   Editing text                Printer idle, Using 4  M:
Main        Pi10   LS1   CR+9   LP5                        Page    1  line  1/54
f1=Actions    f2=Layout    f3=Style    f4=Size    f5=Page    f7=Spell    f8=Options    EXIT
```

Advantages of a Word Processor↵
↵
There are lots of other jobs that you will want your word-
processor to help you with. If you are a Secretary of a club,
then you will want your word-processor to help you circulate
details of forthcoming events or copies of the club newsletter
to members. Or if you are preparing a report on something, then
you will probably have one or more tables to prepare. Or you
might have some sales literature to prepare, which you want to
lay out and style really nicely. ↵

With LocoScript 2, there's essentially endless scope for
revising and styling your text - so much so that you might get
so carried away with producing the perfect document that you
never actually get around to printing it! ↵
↵
Moreover, because you can save your work on disc any time you
like:↵
↵
1) You can start and stop work on a document at will; you don't
have to finish somewhere that is easy to carry on from - like
the bottom of a page - as on a typewriter.↵
↵
2) You can make copies of the document stored on disc,
facilitating easy production of different versions of the same
document with very little extra effort.↵
↵
↵

■ The left- and right-hand ends of the row of dots are
underlined. Put another way, the dots from character position
10 through to 73 are *not* underlined. When you realise that the
underlining marks the width of the **margins** that have been set
for this page, then it becomes clear that the maximum width
of the printed page will equate to the row of dots between the
margins, or in this case 63 characters. As you can see, all the
text lines up with the left margin (10th character position) and
none of the text extends beyond the position of the right
margin. As this text is set to 10 characters per inch (honest!), it
means that the actual printing on the page will not exceed 6.3
inches in width.

■ However, when your type pitch (or spacing) is set to
10 characters per inch then everything works out nice and
neatly on the screen, because that too displays characters
with a spacing of 10 characters per inch. Now you can alter the
spacing for your printout, but you can't change the spacing on
the screen display. So, if you change the spacing for your
printout, the screen display will seem confusing at first.
Try this:

5 Hold down a **[SHIFT]** key and tap the **[f4/f5]** key. The flag menu confirms that the character pitch is set to 10 and you can tell that by the top line and by the tick mark against the number 10 in the second line.

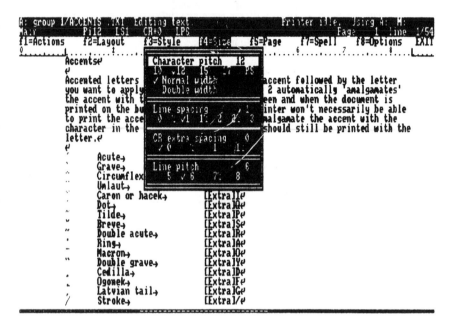

6 Tap once, followed by → once to highlight the number 12 on the second line. Now find the **SET** key (the key marked [+] at the extreme bottom left of the keyboard). Tap this key once to set the character spacing to 12 instead of 10. Notice the top line of the menu and the tick mark on the second line.

7 Tap the **[ENTER]** key to confirm the setting.

8 Tap the key twice to move the text cursor onto the first letter of the second paragraph. Find the key labelled **RELAY/0** in the keypad at the right-hand end of the keyboard (bottom left).

■ SECTION 8

Interpreting the Page display

9 Hold down a **[SHIFT]** key and tap **[RELAY/0]**

The PCW 're-lays-out' the text on the screen at the new character pitch of 12 characters per inch (cpi). On your screen the text seems to extend beyond the right margin, but when it is printed with a 12-cpi print wheel, the printed text will not exceed the 6.4 inches defined by the margin settings.

NOTE Between the row of dots and the Locoscript control area you will see some small right-facing arrows. These mark where TABS have been set for this page. So the part of the display immediately below the Locoscript control area is just like the TAB RACK on a typewriter. On a word processor, it is known as the **ruler line**.

In the text you will also see several symbols which look like backward-facing L-shaped arrows. These mark where the **[RETURN]** key was pressed during the typing of this text. Notice that the symbols do not appear at the end of every line – only at the end of **paragraphs**. The first line of the text on screen is, in fact, a paragraph consisting of a single line.

10 Hold down a **[SHIFT]** key and tap the key (in the second row of the keypad at the right of the keyboard) labelled **[DOC PAGE/8]**.

The text cursor moves to the end of the document. If you look in the top right-hand corner of your screen, on the second line, you will see that the cursor has landed on page 1, line 30 of 54. Notice that all the text now seems to extend beyond the right margin. This demonstrates that when you have changed one of the page settings, the act of *moving the cursor through the text automatically 'RELAYS' the text to the new setting.*

Near the bottom of the screen you will see a broad white line. This marks the bottom of the page you have filled so far.

If you look more closely you will see that the broad white line is not solid. At the left-hand end you will see some black dots and near the middle you will see some black dashes (24 of them). The dots represent lines you have used, whereas the dashes represent unused lines left on the page – that's why there are 24 of them.

Interpreting the Page display

Let us now leave this document and return to the Disk Management Screen by tapping the **[EXIT]** key.

The flag menu offers you four options. All except the second one will get you back to the Disk Management Screen, but in different ways:

■ The first one will save a copy of the file before returning.

■ The second one will save a copy of the file, but remain in the document.

■ The third one will save a copy of your work and then print it.

■ The fourth one will abandon your work, *without saving a copy first*. If you tap **[A]** to select the fourth option, then the **[ENTER]** key to confirm your selection, after a second or so you get back to the Disk Management Screen. But, because you **abandoned** your modifications, the file you have been looking at is not changed in any way.

■ SECTION 9
Keying in text

Starting from the Disk Management Screen:

1 Hold down a **[SHIFT]** key then tap → twice (four times if you have twin drives) and move the groups cursor onto Group 1 on drive M.

2 Tap **[C]** to create a *new* document. The PCW suggests a name for this new file, but it is not very inspiring or memorable, so we will give it a name of our own. (See Section 50.)

3 Key in the file name − **EXAMPLE.TXT** (it does not matter whether you use capitals or lower-case letters, the PCW will convert them to capitals automatically) − and then tap the **[ENTER]** key. After a short pause, the PCW presents you with the blank page display (see Section 8).

4 Key in the following text. **Do not** press the carriage return (the **[RETURN]** key) at all! And do not key in the quotation marks. Keep an eye on the screen as you type the words in:

"**The STEP-BY-STEP series of reference guides provides the average person with an invaluable source of information.**"

5 Tap the **[RETURN]** key twice, to finish the paragraph and to leave a blank line.

6 Now key in:

"**The books assume no prior knowledge of computers – in fact they are specifically designed for the non-specialist who wants to be able to find things out quickly and easily.**"

7 Tap **[RETURN]** and then tap the **[EXIT]** key.

The flag menu offers you four options. All except the second one will get you back to the Disk Management Screen, but in different ways:

SECTION 9
Keying in text

- The first one will save a copy of the file before returning.
- The second one will save a copy of the file, but remain in the document.
- The third one will save a copy of your work and then print it.
- The fourth one will abandon your work, *without saving a copy first*.

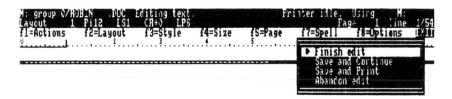

8 Tap **[S]**, then **[P]**, then the **[ENTER]** key. A flag menu shows you some of the printer selections. You can change these if you want to.

9 For now, just tap **[ENTER]** to accept the standard settings. A second flag menu confirms certain things about the printed output and then asks you to confirm that it should proceed.

10 Tap the **[ENTER]** key to proceed.

11 Next you get a warning that the file you have created will be saved on drive M and reminding you to make a permanent copy before switching off the PCW (see Section 7).

12 Acknowledge the warning by tapping the **[ENTER]** key.

The PCW saves a copy of your work, returns to the Disk Management Screen and then seems to stop. But if you look in the column for drive M's group 1 files you'll see one there called **EXAMPLE1.TXT**. Also, if you look in the very top row of the screen you will see that the PCW is politely asking you for paper (for the printer, that is).

■ SECTION 9

Keying in text

13 Put some paper in the printer – lining-up the left-hand side with the **third** rib on the printer casing (see Section 6). If you still have **PCW9512** flashing at the left of the Locoscript control area, tap the **[EXIT]** key to start the print process.

Making a copy of a file in Locoscript

Note If you want to work through this procedure, you will have to work through the previous section first.

The files cursor should be highlighting the name of the file you have just created on drive M. You will know from Section 7 that drive M will not give you a permanent copy of your file. To create a permanent version you will have to make a duplicate copy of the file on drive M and put that duplicate on a disk in drive A (or B if you have it fitted). Here's how you copy a file *from* drive M and put the duplicate on drive A.

1   Tap the **[f4/f3]** key to gain access to Locoscript's file options.

2   The highlighting bar should already be on the 'Copy File' option, so tap the **[ENTER]** key.

3   The next flag menu asks you to pick a destination for the copy, so hold down a **[SHIFT]** key and tap the ← key twice (four times if you have twin drives). Then, still holding down the **[SHIFT]** key, tap ↓ until the groups cursor lands on the **MANUSCRP** group. Then tap the **[ENTER]** key again.

The PCW gives you a chance to change the name of the file if you want to (you would simply key in the new name here). As we do not need to change the name:

4   Just tap **[ENTER]** again. You will see the disk drive work. If, at this point, you get a flag menu on screen telling you that there is an error and that your disk is **write-protected**:

5   Take the disk from the drive and make sure that the small hole at the front left of the disk is covered – you will have to move a small tab either on the left edge or the front edge of the casing. Put the disk back in the drive, tap **[D]** and then **[ENTER]**.

The file name is added to the MANUSCRP column.

■ SECTION 11
Moving the text cursor

Starting from the Disk Management Screen:

1 Move your file cursor onto the file called **DISCINFO** in group 1 on drive A.

2 Tap **[E]** to edit that file. If the details on the flag menu are correct, tap the **[ENTER]** key to get the file on screen.

The PCW displays the text and if you look in the top left-hand corner of the page display you will see the **text cursor** flashing on (or 'under' if that is how you interpret it) the K of 'Keeping'. At the right-hand side of the Locoscript control area (middle row) you'll see that the cursor is on page 1, line 1 of 54.

The text cursor is like the print head on a typewriter — its position determines where the next character you key in will appear on the page. If, for example, you want to change something in the third paragraph, then it is obvious that you will have to move the cursor (or the print head) to the right place on the page before you start.

With a typewriter, you might move the print head to the right place on the page in a number of ways — you might move the paper up manually and then space over with the space bar. Or you might press the carriage return and the space bar. But you can't do that with a word processor — first, because you don't have paper to move and secondly, because tapping the **[RETURN]** key or the **[SPACEBAR]** actually modifies the text.

And that is why you need a range of cursor controls which enable you to move the cursor through the text without changing anything on the way — so let's look at them to see what they do:

1 Look in the pad of keys at the right-hand end of your keyboard and you will see four keys marked with arrows pointing up, down, left and right. Tap → four or five times. Notice that the cursor moves one character to the right each time you tap this key. But also notice that you have a 'ghost' cursor in the **ruler line** (see Section 8). The ghost cursor shows your position *across* the page.

Moving the text cursor

2 Tap ↓ three or four times. This time the ghost cursor does not move, but look in the Locoscript control area − right-hand side of the middle row − and you will see that whereas the ghost cursor tells you how far *across* the page you are, the control area tells you how far *down* the page you are.

The ← and the ↑ work in the same way, i.e. one tap for each character position across or each line up or down the page. But what if you want to move some distance through your work?

3 Hold down a **[SHIFT]** key and, at the same time, tap ↓ twice. This time the cursor moves much further down the page (20 lines for each tap).

So the arrow keys **unshifted** make small movements while the same keys **shifted** make larger movements.

Quite often when you are creating or editing larger documents, you will want to get straight to the end of your text to continue. How do you do it?

4 Hold down a **[SHIFT]** key, then tap the key labelled **[DOC/ PAGE]** (just above the ↑ key).

The PCW will display a message, telling you what it is doing and after a few moments the end of the document appears on screen. Fine. But how do you get back to the beginning again?

5 With the little finger of your left-hand hold down the key labelled **[ALT]** (in the pad of keys at the left-hand end of the keyboard). Then, with the index finger of the same hand, hold down the left **[SHIFT]** key. Now, with your right hand, tap the **[DOC/PAGE]** key again.

6 Tap the **[DOC/PAGE]** key *unshifted* to get to the start of the next page. Now hold down the **[ALT]** key and tap **[DOC/PAGE]** *unshifted* to get back to the start of the previous page.

Moving the text cursor

7 Tap the **[UNIT/PARA]** key twice and watch the cursor move to the start of the next **para**graph each time you tap the key. Now try holding down the **[ALT]** key and then tapping the **[UNIT/PARA]** key twice to get back to where you were.

8 Next, tap the key labelled **[LINE/EOL]**, i.e. line/end-of-line, five times and watch the cursor as it moves to the **end** of the next line each time you tap it. Hold down a **[SHIFT]** key and tap **[LINE/EOL]** to move the cursor to the **start** of the next line. Now hold down **[ALT]** and tap the **[LINE/EOL]** key.

Some general rules are emerging:

■ Tap a key **unshifted** and you get the result which is described by the lower legend on a key.

■ Tap a key **shifted** and you get the upper one.

■ Tap a key (**shifted or unshifted**) together with the **[ALT]** key to reverse the action of the key.

The remaining cursor movement key illustrates the rules:

9 Tap the **[WORD/CHAR]** key a couple of times and you will see that it works just like the → key. Hold down **[ALT]** and tap it and you will see it works like the ← key. Now hold down a **[SHIFT]** key and tap the key and you'll see the cursor move **forward a word at a time**. So, if you hold down **[ALT]** and a **[SHIFT]** key, then tap the **[WORD/CHAR]** key, the cursor must move **backwards a word at a time**.

Some of these cursor controls may seem strange or unnecessary to you at the moment, but as you get more used to word processing with your PCW you will find yourself using them more and more.

The cursor control keys work as I have described *while you are using the Locoscript word-processing software*. They may not behave exactly like this when you are using the PCW without Locoscript.

Moving the text cursor

10 Abandon the file in memory by tapping **[EXIT]**, then **[A]**, then **[ENTER]**.

The disk copy of the file will be unchanged.

PART TWO

Creating and editing documents

■ SECTION 12
Getting rid of unwanted text

Starting from the Disk Management Screen:

1 Move your file cursor onto the filename **diskINFO** in group 1 on the A drive. Tap **[f4/f3]** and then tap **[ENTER]** to confirm that you want to copy the file. Move your groups cursor onto Group 1 on the memory drive (drive M). Tap **[ENTER]** twice to make the copy.

2 Now, tap **[E]** to edit this file, then tap **[ENTER]** to confirm your choice.

No matter how good a typist you are, you will eventually make a mistake of some kind. Now on a typewriter, that might mean starting all over again (if you're anything like me you'll make the mistake on the very last line of an otherwise perfect page!), but with your PCW all you have to do is remove the mistake and then key the text in correctly. The following exercises take you through the various ways you can **delete** text.

Note If your copy of the diskINFO file has been edited before, the exercises might not work precisely as described below. Please make allowances for this or, better still, obtain an unedited copy of the file. We will not be saving any of the changes we make, so you won't damage the file while you are trying things out.

1 I want you to make a change in the sixth line of the second paragraph. So move the cursor down to that line (it starts: "the one you want,").

2 Now move across to the word **your** (using the **[SHIFT]** and the **[WORD/CHAR]** key). It may be just that I have a filthy mind, but that part of the sentence seems less than elegant, so let us change it.

3 With your cursor on the start of the word, tap the **[DEL→]** key (just above the **[RETURN]** key) *five* times to **DEL**ete the word *and* the space after it. Now key in a letter **[a]** followed by a **[space]**. Now move the cursor to the space *after* the word **drawers** and tap the **[←DEL]** key once to delete the letter **s** (one character to the *left* of the cursor).

■ SECTION 12
Getting rid of unwanted text

4 Move the cursor forward a word to the **space** after the word **start**, and key in a letter **[s]**.

That completes the changes, but notice that the line we have been working on is shorter than the others. That is because we have taken out more letters than we have put in. We must put it right.

5 Keep an eye on the screen and tap the **[UNIT/PARA]** key.

Note that as the cursor moves through the document the PCW ensures that the text conforms to the page layout. **This is a general rule!**

6 Tap **[ALT]** and **[DOC/PAGE]** to get back to the start of the page.

7 Tap the **[CUT]** key (in the top row of the pad of keys at the right of the keyboard). The PCW flashes up a reminder of what to do next.

8 Hold down a **[SHIFT]** key and tap **[WORD/CHAR]** five times. You will see that all the text from where you pressed **[CUT]** to the present position of the cursor is highlighted.

■ SECTION 12

Getting rid of unwanted text

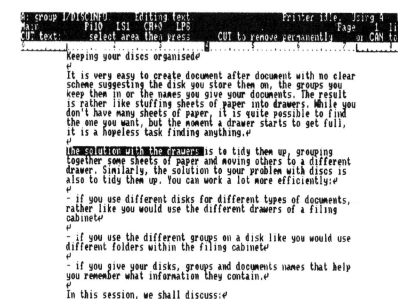

9   Now tap **[CUT]** again.

If you look closely you will see that the PCW has *cut* or deleted everything that had been highlighted **including the carriage return symbol**.

10   Tap **[DOC/PAGE]**, then hold down the **[ALT]** key and tap **[UNIT/PARA]** twice (you should land on the letter 'E' of 'Every operation is').

11   Tap **[CUT]** and then **[UNIT/PARA]** twice. Then tap **[CUT]** again and watch as the PCW deletes line-by-line the text you have marked, at the same time *pulling* all the other text up to fill the gap that would otherwise have been left there.

■ SECTION 12

Getting rid of unwanted text

You will know that the broad line across the screen represents the end of the page. What we have done here is to pull text from page two and put it on page one. You may not want that to happen, so see Section 29 for details of how to *force* a page break to occur just where you want.

12 Move the cursor down to the second line on page two (the one that starts with the words "information, specified by its capacity"). Then move across to the 'I' of 'If it has been...'. Tap [CUT], then move the cursor down two lines (notice the highlighting). Finally move the cursor left to the space after the full stop and before the word 'If'. Then tap [CUT] again and watch the screen.

Once again we have made a mess of our layout, but we can soon put it right.

13 Tap the [UNIT/PARA] key and watch the screen.

So the PCW enables you to delete text a character at a time, but it allows you to cut words, lines, paragraphs, or pages in one go.

14 Abandon the file in memory by tapping [EXIT], then [A], then tapping [ENTER].

The disk copy of the file will be unchanged.

■ SECTION 13

Inserting letters and words

Starting from the Disk Management Screen:

1 Move your file cursor onto the file named **DISCINFO** in Group 1 on drive A. Tap **[f4/f3]** and then tap **[ENTER]** to confirm that you want to copy the file. Move your groups cursor onto Group 1 on drive M. Tap **[ENTER]** twice to make the copy.

2 Now, tap **[E]** to edit this file followed by **[ENTER]** to confirm your choice.

The first line of text in this file seems to be intended as a sub-heading, but it looks just the same as the rest of the text. How can we make it stand out more? Try this:

3 Tap the **[SHIFT LOCK]** key (you should see the little red light come on). Now, key in the words **SECTION ONE:** followed by two **spaces**. You will see the first line of the text move down to make room for the words you keyed in. It looks as if your text is on a different line from the original.

4 Tap the **[UNIT/PARA]** key and watch what happens. The layout adjusts itself. So the 'two-line' look you had just now was purely a temporary measure designed to give you as much space as you wanted.

5 Move the cursor across to the word **with** in the first line of the second paragraph (use **[SHIFT]** and **[WORD/CHAR]**). Now key in the words **after document** followed by a space. *Watch the screen closely as you do so.*

6 Now tap **[UNIT/PARA]** again.

So you can now see that you can insert letters and words at your will. To see how to insert much larger lumps of text, see Section 14 following.

7 Abandon the file in memory by tapping **[EXIT]**, then **[A]**, followed by **[ENTER]**.

The disk copy of the file will be unchanged.

Inserting blocks of text into a document

Starting from the Disk Management Screen:

1 Move your groups cursor down one and then across to Group 1 on drive M. Tap **[C]** and then **[ENTER]** to create a new document with the name that the PCW suggests.

The blank page display tells you that the PCW is waiting for your 'input'. In this section I want to show you how to construct a document with the absolute minimum of typing.

2 Tap the **[f2/f1]** key. The third item on the flag menu that appears is **Insert text**, which is what we want to do.

3 Select **Insert text** (either by tapping the letter **[I]** or by moving the highlighting bar), then tap the **[ENTER]** key.

The PCW displays that looks like the normal Disk Management Screen, but if you look at the top line of the control area you will see it says: "**Editing text**".

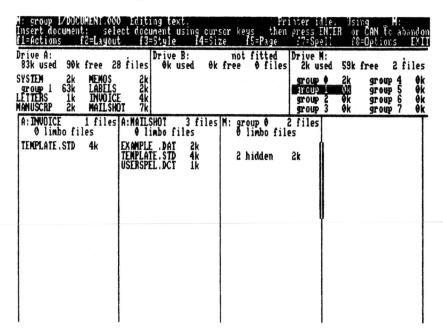

■ SECTION 14

Inserting blocks of text into a document

4 Move the groups cursor onto Group 1 on drive A. When the screen settles, move the file cursor onto the file called **MISTAKE.EG** to select that file as the one to be inserted into our empty document.

If you were to edit MISTAKE.EG, you would see that it is fourteen lines long, set up with margins at the 10th and the 50th character positions, i.e. the text is not more than 40 characters wide. Watch what happens as you insert it into *this* document.

5 Tap the **[ENTER]** key twice to confirm your selection. The PCW reads the disk and loads a copy of MISTAKE.EG into the page on screen (the copy on the disk is still there, unchanged).

Ignore the spelling for the moment! But notice that the file takes up only 12 lines here. That is because the PCW automatically adjusted the text to fit the layout for your new file (here the text has a maximum width of 62 characters).

6 Tap the **[RETURN]** key a couple of times and now insert another (longer) document. Tap **[f2/f1]**, then **[I]**, followed by the **[ENTER]** key. Notice that the groups cursor is on drive M again and not where you left it when you selected the file to be inserted.

7 Move the groups cursor back onto Group 1 on drive A. Then move the file cursor onto the **DISCINFO** file. Tap **[ENTER]** twice to select and read the file into your document.

You have created a new document more than two pages in length and yet you have keyed in no text at all. Of course, *someone* had to type the text in the first place, but even so you can see the value of being able to read in text. It means you will only have to type, say, a standard paragraph for a quotation once and you can use it over and over again. See also Section 17 for some other aspects of this same principle.

8 Abandon the file in memory by tapping **[EXIT]**, then **[A]**, then **[ENTER]**.

■ SECTION 15

Finding a word (or words) in the text

The ability to **find** certain sections of the text is one that has many uses. Once you know how to do it – and once you realise how easy it is – you will be able to devise your own procedures.

Starting from the Disk Management Screen:

1   Move your files cursor to the right and then down until it settles on the file **DISCINFO** in group 1 on drive A. Tap **[f4/f3]** and then tap **[ENTER]** to confirm that you want to copy the file. Move your groups cursor onto Group 1 on arive M. Tap **[ENTER]** twice to make the copy.

2   Now, tap **[E]** to edit this file, followed by **[ENTER]** to confirm your choice.

3   Once you have the text on screen, tap the key labelled **[EXCH/FIND]** (in the second row of the pad of keys on the right of your keyboard).

The flag menu is asking you to key in the text you want to find and it is also offering you some alternative ways of carrying out the search. The PCW assumes that you want it to ignore the 'case' of the text, i.e. you don't mind if it looks for the text in capitals or in lower case. It also assumes that you don't want to look just for whole words, i.e. if the text you key in occurs within a larger word it will point that out for you; that you will not be using **wildcards**, i.e. that you will not be using a specific character to represent another (see below) and it assumes you will want to continue with the search. The best way to understand all that is to work through some examples.

4   Key in the word **sing** and tap the **[ENTER]** key to continue with the search.

The PCW searches through all the text on screen, then scrolls the text up until it finds the first occurrence of our text in the word **using** on the first line of the second page.

5   Tap **[EXCH/FIND]** again and you will repeat the search, so tap the **[ENTER]** key.

This time our text appears within the word **Single**. Notice it starts with a capital S, but the text we supplied for the search did not.

6 Tap **[EXCH/FIND]** once more and tap **[ENTER]**. Then repeat the process for the final time for this search.

7 Now hold down **[ALT]** and a **[SHIFT]** key and then tap **[DOC/PAGE]** to get back to the start of the file.

A search always goes forward from the position of the cursor, so on short documents like this it is a good idea to start the search from the beginning of the file.

8 Tap **[EXCH/FIND]** and delete the text we keyed in for the previous search with the **[DEL→]** key. Now key in **dis?** (note the question mark — this is the **wildcard** symbol I mentioned earlier). Then move the black bar on the menu down to the line which says **Use wildcards**. Tap the **SET** key (the key marked **[+]** at the bottom left of the keyboard). The tick against the option, shows it is set ON.

9 Tap the **[ENTER]** key to continue with the search.

The PCW has found the word **disks**. This matches the 'mask' we supplied for the search — which was, **d i s something**.

10 Tap **[EXCH/FIND]** again, followed by **[ENTER]**.

This time the PCW has found the word **disk** which, of course, still matches our mask.

Hint If you want to delete your text a sentence at a time (see also Section 12), you can speed up the process by using the FIND procedure and the CUT procedure in combination.

11 Hold down **[ALT]** and **[SHIFT]** and tap **[DOC/PAGE]** (to get back to the start of the file for our example). Tap the **[CUT]** key. Now tap **[EXCH/FIND]**. Delete the text in the top line of the flag menu and then key in a full stop. Watch the screen and tap **[ENTER]**. Now tap **[CUT]** again. Use **[DEL→]** to tidy up.

12 Now abandon the file with **[EXIT]**, **[A]**, **[ENTER]**.

■ SECTION 16
Finding and exchanging text

The ability to find and replace certain sections of the text is one that has many uses. Once you know how to do it — and once you realise how easy it is — you will be able to devise your own procedures.

Starting from the Disk Management Screen:

1 Move your files cursor to the right and then down until it settles on **DISCINFO** in Group 1 on drive A. Tap **[f4/f3]** and then tap **[ENTER]** to confirm that you want to copy the file. Move your groups cursor onto Group 1 on drive M. Tap **[ENTER]** twice to make the copy.

2 Now tap **[E]** to edit this file followed by **[ENTER]** to confirm your choice.

3 Once the text is on screen, hold down a **[SHIFT]** key and tap the key labelled **[EXCH/FIND]** (in the second row of the pad of keys on the right of your keyboard).

The flag menu is asking you to key in the text you want to find and what you want to replace it with. It is also offering you some alternative ways of carrying out the search and exchange procedure (see the previous section).

4 Key in the word to FIND as **disk**, then move the highlighting bar down a line on the menu (with the ↓). Key in the replacement word **disc** so we end up with that spelling throughout the file.

In the bottom section of the flag menu you will see that the PCW has assumed that you want to make a manual exchange, rather than an automatic exchange. We will accept this setting.

5 Tap the **[ENTER]** key to begin the procedure.

A flag menu gives you three options now:

■ If you tap the **SET** key (marked **[+]**), the PCW will make the exchange.

■ If you were to tap the **CLEAR** key, marked **[−]** (next to the Set key), the PCW would not make an exchange, but simply move on to find the next occurrence.

■ If you were to tap the [CAN] key, the PCW would cancel (abandon) the activity.

6 Tap the Set key ([+]) to make the exchange.

Notice that while the 'Match Found' flag is on the screen, you lose the text cursor, so it is impossible to tell where the match is. Here it doesn't matter because we are pretty sure that we want to change all occurrences, *but* there will often be times when you will *not* want to change every one. The solution is to wait for a few seconds until the flag menu disappears and the text cursor reappears.

7 Carry on making the changes until you get to the end of the file. Then hold down [ALT] and one of the [SHIFT] keys. At the same time tap the key labelled [DOC/PAGE] to return to the beginning of the document.

8 Hold down a [SHIFT] key and tap [EXCH/FIND]. This time we will get the PCW to change *every* occurrence of **disk** to **disc**. Move the text cursor on the menu across to the **k** in **disk** on the first line. Tap [DEL→] once to get rid of the **k**. Then key in a letter **c**. Now move down a line with the ↓ key and change **disk** to **disc**.

9 This time we want an automatic exchange, so move the highlighting bar down to the bottom of the flag menu and notice that as the bar moves from 'Manual exchange' to 'Automatic exchange', the arrowhead moves with the bar. So just moving the bar to that line has switched the facility on. Tap the [ENTER] key and watch as the PCW riffles through the text making changes as it goes.

So that is how you find and substitute words with your PCW.

10 Abandon the file in memory by tapping [EXIT], then [A], followed by [ENTER].

The disk copy of the file will be unchanged.

■ SECTION 17
Handling blocks of text

On many occasions you will want to make changes to quite large sections, i.e. **blocks** of text. Your PCW equips you to do three things with such blocks: you can **copy** a block, **move** a block, or you can **delete** a block. The procedure you follow is essentially the same for each activity, with only minor but critical changes for each manoeuvre. You carry out block activities with the three keys in the top row of the keypad at the right of the keyboard: **CUT**, **COPY** and **PASTE**.

The following examples will illustrate each of the procedures. Start in each case from the Disk Management Screen.

Copying a block

1   Begin by moving your files cursor to the file named **PCWINFO** in Group 1 drive A.

2   Tap the **[f4/f3]** key and tap **[ENTER]** to copy the file. When prompted, move the groups cursor to group 1 on drive M and tap **[ENTER]** twice to make the copy.

3   Tap **[E]** and then **[ENTER]** to edit this file.

Before you can work with a block you have to tell the PCW what you intend to do and which parts of the text will comprise the block you will be manipulating. If you intend to delete the block you would start by tapping the **[CUT]** key, but if you were intending to copy or move the block you would start by tapping the **[COPY]** key.

4   Tap the **[COPY]** key.

A flag menu reminds you to mark the text and prompts you to tap the **[CUT]** key if you want to remove the text from the page. If you want to leave it on the page, but take a copy of it to duplicate elsewhere then you would press **[COPY]** again.

5   Watch the screen and tap the **[DOC/PAGE]** key.

Handling blocks of text

As the cursor moves to the start of the next page, it marks the text for you. You will move that text elsewhere – which means you will need to 'cut' it from here and 'paste' it in somewhere else.

6 Now tap [CUT] and then in response to the prompt, give this block the number **1** by tapping the number [1] key in the top row of your keyboard. The marked text slides away, but you still have a copy of it.

7 Tap the [f2/f1] key, then key in [s] (show blocks) and tap [ENTER].

Against the number 1 in the list you'll see the first few characters of the block you have saved.

8 Tap the [CAN] key to cancel the flag display. Now, tap the [RETURN] key a couple of times and then tap the [PASTE] key, followed by the number [1] to paste your block into this new position.

Once you have saved a block in memory like this it will stay there until you RESET your computer, so you can call it up over and over again if you want to. Like this:

1 Tap [PASTE] and the number [1] again.

To summarise so far: If you have decided to either **move** or **copy** (duplicate) a block of text, start by tapping the [COPY] key, then mark the text and give the block a number. Move the cursor to the point in the text where you want the block inserted and then **PASTE** it into position.

Deleting a block

To **delete** a block is a simpler, though similar process:

1 Tap the [CUT] key. Now tap [ALT] [SHIFT] and [DOC/PAGE] (this time you are not asked to provide a number, because you are CUTTING and discarding text). Now tap [CUT] again and watch the text slither away.

Handling blocks of text

The block you originally marked is still stored as block number 1, so you can paste it back in if you want to. In fact it stays in memory until you either give another block the same number or you RESET your system.

Working with phrases

So you have seen the essential points about working with **blocks** of text, but the PCW also allows you to call up standard **phrases** and paste them in. How are they different? The principal difference is that **phrases** are loaded into memory when you start up your system, so they are available all the time. But you also use and save them differently.

1 Tap the **[PASTE]** key and then key in the letter **[Z]**. The PCW goes to its phrases library and reads in the (longish) phrase it knows as 'phrase Z'. So what other phrases are available to you now?

2 Tap the **[f2/f1]** key and then tap the letter **[S]** to highlight 'Show phrases'. Then tap **[ENTER]**.

Those are the phrases which have already been set up for you. The line of arrows at the bottom of the flag display means tap ↓ to see more. As you have seen, you can call up any of those phrases simply by tapping the **[PASTE]** key followed by the relevant letter key.

3 Tap **[CAN]** to cancel the 'phrases' display.

When you want to set up your own library of phrases, look in Session 15 (around page 180) of your Amstrad PCW9512 User Instructions Book.

4 Abandon the file in memory by tapping **[EXIT]** then **[A]**, followed by **[ENTER]**.

The disk copy of the file will be unchanged.

■ SECTION 18
Checking your spelling

You can check your spelling in two ways:

■ You can either check a single word, while you are editing, or

■ You can check the whole of a document in one separate process.

Let's look at checking a single word. Start, as usual, from the Disk Management Screen, but in loading the Locoscript files into memory, notice how long it takes to copy the .**DCT** (dictionary) files into memory − and, therefore, how big they must be.

1 Begin by moving your files cursor to the file named **DISCINFO** in Group 1 on drive A.

2 Tap the **[f4/f3]** key and tap **[ENTER]** to copy the file. When prompted, move the groups cursor to Group 1 on drive M and tap **[ENTER]** twice to make the copy.

3 Tap **[E]** and then **[ENTER]** to edit this file.

4 Tap the **[UNIT/PARA]** key twice to get to the third paragraph which starts 'The solution with…'.

5 Move across the page to the letter **i** in **solution**. Tap the **[DEL→]** key once to delete the **i**. Now we know that we have a spelling mistake to work with.

6 Hold down a **[SHIFT]** key and then tap the key labelled **[SPCHK]** (between the ← and the → keys).

The word where your cursor was is highlighted. You then see a flag display of part of the dictionary, with the suspect word in the top line of the flag. The words below that are ones that are close to the word in question. The list is fairly long because the PCW doesn't know which part of the word (if any) is wrong. The correct word, **solution** is about half way down the list. It confirms that the word is not right. So how do you correct it?

7 Move the black bar down to the word **solution** (with the ↓) and then tap the **[ENTER]** key. Watch the text adjust itself as the correct word is inserted and the cursor reappears at the end of the corrected word.

■ SECTION 19

Checking a complete document for spelling

First we will have to put in a couple of spelling mistakes for the PCW to find.

1 Tap the **[DOC/PAGE]** key to get to the start of page two. Move across to the word **using** in the first line of the second page and delete the letter **u**. Then move down three lines and to the right, so you end up on the word **operations**. Delete the letter **e** in this word.

2 Now hold down the **[ALT]** key and a **[SHIFT]** key and then tap **[DOC/PAGE]** to return to the start of the file.

If you look at the bottom line of the Locoscript control area you will see a row of **function key** activities that are open to you now. You will notice that **f7 = Spell**. This is the main spelling check procedure.

3 Tap the **[f8/f7]** key.

The flag menu offers you four options:

■ Check the whole of the document from the start.

■ Check forwards through the rest of the document from the cursor position.

■ Check the word that the cursor is on (like the **[SPCHK]** key).

■ Edit your own dictionary.

4 The highlighting bar is on the option we want, so tap **[ENTER]**.

You will see the text display riffle and you will hear the disk drive work and then everything seems to stop. But if you look in the Locoscript control area (at the right-hand side) you will see that the PCW is checking the text line by line. The text scrolls up as the PCW finishes checking the text on screen and then the cursor stops to highlight a word and a flag menu appears.

■ SECTION 19

Checking a complete document for spelling

The PCW has completely missed the first mistake, which is not really surprising, because the word we left in the text is a valid word — **sing**. The PCW can't tell if a word has been used in the wrong place. It checks only that each word in the text matches a word in the dictionaries. So the sentence, **cat the sat mat the on**, would be perfectly acceptable, even though it ends in a preposition!

The flag menu is telling you it has stopped the checking process at the word **oprations** — which does not match a dictionary. It suggests that you might want to replace the word with **operations** — which is the closest match it can find. You need not accept its suggestion. The lower half of the flag menu offers you seven different courses of action at this point. But here, we do want to accept the PCW's suggestion and that option is highlighted, so:

Checking a complete document for spelling

5 Tap the **[ENTER]** key and the PCW replaces the word for you and continues checking. Tap the **[STOP]** key (top left of the main keyboard) as we are pretty sure that there are no more mistakes, so there's no point in checking further. Then tap the **[STOP]** key a second time, read the message from LocoSpell, and tap the **[ENTER]** key.

6 Abandon the file in memory by tapping **[EXIT]**, **[A]**, followed by **[ENTER]**.

The disk copy of the file will be unchanged.

■ SECTION 20
Getting rid of an unwanted file

DO NOT USE your master Locoscript 2 disk for this section. You should anyway be using a working copy (see Sections 1 and 4). Start from the Disk Management Screen:

1   First we will copy a file so we can make a deletion without disturbing things too much. Move your files cursor onto the file called **LETTER.1** (Group 1, drive A).

2   As we intend to work on a FILE, tap **[f4/f3]**. Make a mental note of that flag menu; we will be coming back to it.

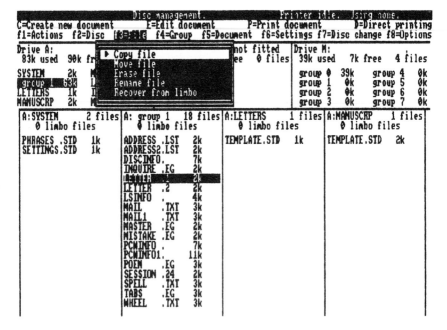

3   Tap **[ENTER]** to copy the file we have selected. Then move the files cursor one column to the right (to the 'A:LETTERS' column) and tap **[ENTER]** again.

4   Alter the name of the file, i.e. give it a *new* name) by keying in **letter** followed by two of your initials, e.g. for me the file name would end up as **LETTERJC.1**).

Getting rid of an unwanted file

5 Tap [ENTER] to make the copy.

You will see and hear the disk drive work, then you will see your new file appear in the A:LETTERS column. (Notice that the original file is still there). Now we are ready to try erasing a whole file.

Check that the cursor is still highlighting the file you have just created, because you start the erasing process by selecting the file that you want to get rid of. Now, **erasing, copying, moving, renaming and recovering from limbo** (more about that below) are all things you can do to **files**. So:

6 Tap [f4/f3] (files options function key). You get that same flag menu I asked you to make a mental note about.

7 Tap [E] to move the highlighting bar to the 'Erase file' option, followed by [ENTER].

The PCW checks that you really do want to erase that file. (If you have selected the wrong one, or if you change your mind, just tap the [CAN] key here to cancel the activity). If you want to go ahead:

8 Tap the [ENTER] key.

The PCW mutters to itself for a moment and then your file disappears from the screen. *But*, notice that at the top of the column it now says that this column holds '1 limbo files'. So what is a **limbo file**?

When you erase a file with Locoscript it does not discard the file completely at first. If there is space on the disk it puts 'erased' files into a special 'limbo' category. However as the disk fills up these limbo files will be overwritten by new files, so you can't depend on a file staying in limbo for ever. You can tell the PCW to display limbo files if you want to see them. In fact, if you want to erase a limbo file you must display its name first. So:

Getting rid of an unwanted file

9 Hold down a **[SHIFT]** key and tap the **[f8/f7]** key. As the first option on the flag menu, 'Show Limbo files' is highlighted, tap the **[SET]** key (**[+]**) to put a tick mark against that setting and then tap the **[ENTER]** key.

After three or four seconds you will see your file reappear on the screen. But notice that this time the file name and size is followed by **lim**...(limbo).

```
                    Disc management.                Printer idle.  Using none.
C=Create new document      E=Edit document      P=Print document      D=Direct printing
f1=Actions   f2=Disc   f3=File   f4=Group   f5=Document   f6=Settings  f7=Disc change f8=Options

Drive A:                        Drive B:        not fitted  Drive M:
83k used   90k free  28 files   0k used  0k free  0 files   2k used   60k free   2 files

SYSTEM     2k   MEMOS      2k                              group 0   2k    group 4   0k
  group 1 63k   LABELS     2k                              group 1   0k    group 5   0k
████████████   INVOICE    4k                              group 2   0k    group 6   0k
MANUSCRP   2k   MAILSHOT   7k                              group 3   0k    group 7   0k

A:SYSTEM     2 files A: group 1  18 files A:LETTERS     1 files A:MANUSCRP    1 files
  0 limbo files        0 limbo files       1 limbo files          0 limbo files

PHRASES .STD  1k   ADDRESS .LST  2k   ██████████████  TEMPLATE.STD   2k
SETTINGS.STD  1k   ADDRESS2.LST  2k   TEMPLATE.STD  1k
                   DISCINFO.      7k
                   INQUIRE .EG   2k
                   LETTER  .1    2k
                   LETTER  .2    2k
                   LSINFO        4k
                   MAIL    .TXT  3k
                   MAIL1   .TXT  3k
                   MASTER  .EG   2k
                   MISTAKE .EG   2k
                   PCWINFO.      7k
                   PCWINFO1.    11k
                   POEM    .EG   3k
                   SESSION .24   2k
                   SPELL   .TXT  3k
                   TABS    .EG   3k
                   WHEEL   .TXT  3k
```

Let us get rid of that **lim** file once and for all:

10 Move the files cursor onto the limbo file and tap the familiar **[f4/f3]** key. Tap **[E]** for Erase, and then tap **[ENTER]**. Confirm that you want to erase the file by tapping **[ENTER]** again.

The display updates and you will notice that there are now '0 limbo files' in the A:LETTERS column.

Creating a letter

Start from the Disk Management Screen, then, as we are going to create a letter:

1 Move your files cursor into the A:LETTERS column and tap **[C]**.

You would not normally put your document files on this disk — you would create a separate data disk — but, we will work on the same disk here because I cannot be certain that you have in fact created a separate data disk (see page 10 of the Amstrad PCW9512 User Instructions).

The PCW will offer you a very unhelpful file name, so the first thing to do is to think of a more useful name for the file (see Section 50).

2 Overtype the existing file name with **AUTOBOOK.LET**. If you hit a wrong key by mistake, just use the **[←DEL]** key to delete the bit that's wrong and key it in again. Notice that it doesn't matter whether you key in the letters in upper or lower case. The PCW will automatically display capitals on the screen.

3 Tap the **[ENTER]** key to open the new file and to get the 'blank' page display (see Section 8).

You will see that this page display has margins set at column 10 and at column 72, so the printed text will have a maximum width of 6.2 inches if you print out at 10 characters per inch (cpi), and it will have a maximum width of just over 5 inches if you print out at 12 cpi (see Section 23). Notice also that three tabs have been defined for this page layout.

4 For this exercise I want you to key in the sample letter below. As usual, the words in **bold** print and in square brackets tell you which keys to hit and when.

5 If you hit a wrong key by mistake, just use the **[←DEL]** key to delete the bit that's wrong and key it in again.

6 In your own time, have a go at creating the letter.

■ SECTION 21
Creating a letter

SAMPLE LETTER

[TAB][TAB]PRIVATE AND CONFIDENTIAL[**RETURN**]
[**RETURN**]
The Manager[**RETURN**]
Hereford Cattle Bank[**RETURN**]
Crossways[**RETURN**]
HEREFORD[**RETURN**]
M00 4T[**RETURN**]
[**RETURN**]
[**RETURN**]
[**RETURN**]
Date:[**TAB**] January 3 1988[**RETURN**]
[**RETURN**]
[**RETURN**]
[**RETURN**]
Dear Sir,[**RETURN**]
[TAB][TAB][TAB]YOUR LETTER DATED DECEMBER 31[**RETURN**]
[**RETURN**]
I am sorry. It will not happen again. Cross my heart![**RETURN**]
[**RETURN**]
I must say that it is amazing how expensive Christmas is getting
nowadays. It must stop soon don't you think?[**RETURN**]
[**RETURN**]
Yours faithfully[**RETURN**]

(text ends)

7 When you have checked your work, tap the **[EXIT]** key
followed by **[S]** and **[P]** (watch the highlighting bar on
the menu).

8 Put a sheet of paper in the printer (see Section 23). Then
tap **[ENTER]**. You will notice **PCW9512** flashing at the left
of the Locoscript control area.

9 Tap the **[EXIT]** key to continue. The PCW saves the work
you have done and ther. displays a flag menu which
describes what it is about to do.

Creating a letter

10 For now, just tap **[ENTER]** to accept the standard print procedure and tap **[ENTER]** again to accept the standard print settings.

11 When the printer has finished, remove the paper and have a look at your finished work.

Creating a report/thesis/book

A report, a thesis, or a book is different from a letter in two main ways:

■ First, the size of the finished document.

■ Secondly, the fact that the layout conventions are much more open to individual interpretation.

We therefore need a page layout that gives us maximum freedom. So, Starting from the Disk Management Screen:

1 Move your files cursor into the A:MANUSCRP column and then tap **[C]**.

You would not normally put your document files on this disk — you would create a separate data disk — but we will work on the same disk here because I cannot be certain that you have, in fact, created a separate data disk (see page 10 of the Amstrad PCW9512 User Instructions).

The PCW will offer you a very unhelpful file name, so the first thing to do is to think of a more useful name for the file (see Section 50).

2 Tap the → key and move the cursor in the first line of the flag menu onto the space *after* the dot in the file name. Key in two of your initials and then tap **[DEL→]** to delete the spare character.

If you hit a wrong key by mistake, just use the **[←DEL]** key to delete the bit that's wrong and key it in again. Notice that it doesn't matter whether you key in the letters in upper or lower case. The PCW will automatically display capitals on the screen. In my case the file name would end up as **DOCUMENT.JC**.

3 Tap the **[ENTER]** key to open the new file and to get the 'blank' page display (see Section 8).

You will see that this page display has margins set at column 10 and at column 72, so the printed text will have a maximum width of 6.2 inches if you print out at 10 characters per inch (cpi), and it will have a maximum width of just over 5 inches if you print out at 12 cpi (see Section 23). Notice also that five tabs have been defined for this page layout.

■ SECTION 22
Creating a report/thesis/book

The text that appears on screen describes how you should use this page layout (**document TEMPLATE**). The last paragraph may be a bit puzzling. The best way to illustrate what it means is to go through the steps involved in setting up a document such as this:

1   Tap the **[f2/f1]** key. Accept the 'Document setup' option by tapping the **[ENTER]** key.

```
 LETTERS /DOCUMENT.DC   Document setup.              Printer idle.  Using A:  M:
Pagination   P110   LS1   CB+0   LP5                           Page ---- line --/54
f1=Actions  f2=Layout  f3=Style  f4=Size  f5=Page  f6=Printing  f7=Spell  f8=Options  EXIT
```

```
━━━end of header 1 : used for all pages━━━━━━━━━━━━━━━━━━━━━━━━━━━━━━
━━━end of footer 1 : used for all pages━━━━━━━━━━━━━━━━━━━━━━━━━━━━━━
━━━end of header 2 : used for no pages at all━━━━━━━━━━━━━━━━━━━━━━━━
━━━end of footer 2 : used for no pages at all━━━━━━━━━━━━━━━━━━━━━━━━
```

The display you see on the screen first may seem rather a muddle. You need to note firstly that it mentions **headers** and **footers** and it mentions odd and even pages. Headers and footers are sections of text that will be printed at the head and the foot of each page in the document, and you can arrange things so the headers and footers on even numbered pages are different from those on odd numbered pages. So, you can specify four different sections of text. The on-screen display shows you what those four sections of text are now. The idea is that you edit this layout to suit yourself.

2   Hold down a **[SHIFT]** key and tap the **[EXCH/FIND]** key. Tell the PCW to find **Book Title**.

3   Move the cursor down one line on the menu and then key in the name of the file you are creating – **DOCUMENT. (your initials)**.

4   Move the highlighting bar down to 'Automatic exchange' and tap **[ENTER]**.

Now, when you print the document we are about to create, the file name will be printed at the bottom of each page (actually there will be only one page to print, but that will be enough).

5 Tap **[EXIT]** followed by **[ENTER]**. Now tap the **[CUT]** key, followed by the **[DOC/PAGE]** key, followed by **[CUT]** again to get rid of the text on screen.

6 For this exercise I want you to key in the sample text that appears on the next page. As usual, the words in **bold** print and in square brackets tell you which keys to hit and when.

7 If you hit a wrong key by mistake, just use the **[←DEL]** key to delete the bit that's wrong and key it in again.

```
A:LETTERS /DOCUMENT.CC   Editing text.              Printer idle. Using A: M:
Main        Pi10  LS1   CR+0  LP6                        Page    1  line 23/54
f1=Actions      f2=Layout    f3=Style    f4=Size    f5=Page    f7=Spell    f8=Options    EXIT
0........1.......2.......3.......4.......5.......6.......7...L.......8.......
                          SOME NEW TEXT↵
↵
I am keying in this text simply to explore the way that the
"MANUSCRP" layout can be used for writing large documents.
These meagre lines will have to represent my novel or my
expenses claim or whatever.↵
↵
I particularly like the way that I can use the tabs to indent
text. For example, you can indent:↵
↵
  →   Sub-sections↵
↵
  →   →   Sub Sub-sections↵
↵
  →   →   →   Sub Sub Sub-sections↵
↵
all the way through to a totally ridiculous situation. But you
never know..!↵
↵
By the way I notice that the text I have keyed in is  laid  out
with its right hand edge lined up the right margin. Does  that
mean that my ideas about the world will be justified..?↵
■
```

SAMPLE TEXT

[+][C][E]SOME NEW TEXT**[RETURN]**
[RETURN]
I am keying in this text simply to explore the way that
the "MANUSCRP" layout can be used for writing large
documents. These meager lines will have to represent
my novel or my expenses claim or whatever.**[RETURN]**
[RETURN]
I particularly like the way that I can use the tabs to

indent text. For example, you can indent:**[RETURN]**
[RETURN]
[TAB]Sub-sections**[RETURN]**
[RETURN]
[TAB][TAB]Sub Sub-sections**[RETURN]**
[RETURN]
[TAB][TAB][TAB]Sub Sub Sub-sections**[RETURN]**
[RETURN]
all the way through to a totally ridiculous situation.
But you never know!**[RETURN]**
[RETURN]
By the way, I notice that the text I have keyed in is
laid out with its right-hand edge lined up the right
margin. Does this mean that my ideas about the world
will be justified ?**[RETURN]**

(text ends)

8 When you have checked your work, tap the **[EXIT]** key
followed by **[S]** and **[P]** (watch the highlighting bar on
the menu).

9 Put a sheet of paper in the printer (see Section 23). Then
tap **[ENTER]**. You will notice **PCW9512** flashing at the left
of the Locoscript control area.

10 Tap the **[EXIT]** key to continue. The PCW saves the work
you have done and then displays a flag menu which
describes what it is about to do.

11 For now, just tap **[ENTER]** to accept the standard print
procedure and tap **[ENTER]** again to accept the standard
print settings.

12 Wait for the printer to print the footer for the page! When
the printer has finished, remove the paper and have a look
at your finished work.

■ SECTION 23
Printing a document

The PCW has two main printing procedures. If you have worked through either of the two previous sections in this chapter you will have seen the first: saving your work and then immediately printing **the file you have just created or edited**. The second print procedure is very similar, but much more flexible in that you can print **any document you like**. In this section we will be looking at the second procedure.

The PCW has a set of standard printing settings – which you can alter if you want to. We shall be examining the main changes you might want to make, but first, the standard printing process.

Starting from the Disk Management Screen:

1 Start by moving your files cursor onto the document we want to print. In this case, move the files cursor onto INQUIRE.EG (Group 1, drive A) and tap **[P]** (for print).

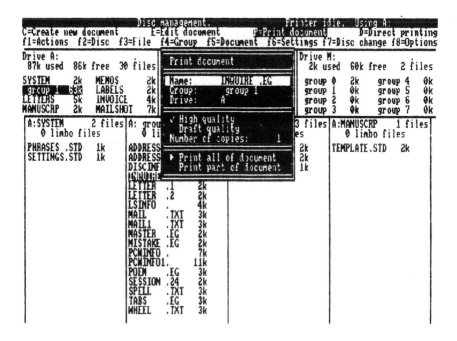

■ SECTION 23
Printing a document

The flag menu tells you that the PCW is about to print the document it describes in high-quality print and it will produce one copy of the complete document. So this menu describes **what** the PCW is about to print.

If you have the standard PCW9512 printer and no other, you have no option but to accept the high-quality setting. But if you install a dot-matrix printer into your PCW system, you will be able to select either **draft** (higher speed) printouts, or **high quality**.

2 Move the highlighting bar down the menu to the 'Number of copies' line, and tap the number **[2]**. Then tap **[ENTER]** to confirm this setting and tap **[ENTER]** again to tell the PCW to go ahead.

The next flag menu tells you **how** the PCW is about to print your document — in other words the standard settings for your version of Locoscript 2.

3 Put a sheet of your standard typing paper in the printer (see below).

4 First, check that the printer's **tractor feed** (for continuous stationery) is *not* fitted. (If it is fitted, remove it by unclipping the front edge and then lift and "hinge" the unit backwards, so that the two hooks at the back of the unit clear their locating holes.) Fit the paper tray.

5 Take a sheet of your typing paper and slip it gently between the casing of the printer and the back surface of the printer platen (the black rubber roller). Line-up the left-hand edge of the paper with the third rib on the printer casing.

Towards the right-hand end of the platen you will see two levers. The one to the rear of the platen is the **paper release lever**; the one just in front of the platen is the **paper load lever**.

Printing a document

6 Move the paper load lever towards the front of the printer to its *fullest* extent. This lever has two positions and you should move it through the first 'stop' to the second. Then let it return about a third of the way back to the first 'stop'. The printer will now feed your paper in, leaving it in position ready for you to start printing.

7 If you want to adjust the position of the paper, move the paper release lever towards the front of the printer. This will allow you to move the paper into the right position.

8 When you have finished adjusting your paper, reset the paper release lever *and* the paper load lever.

9 Tap [**ENTER**] to tell the PCW to proceed.

When you load the printer the PCW assumes that you may want to make a number of adjustments to the printer, so it automatically goes into its **printer control state** (or MODE). If you look at the three bright lines at the top of the screen you will see that they have changed (notice particularly that **PCW9512** is flashing at the left of the second line).

10 For our purposes now, just tap the [**EXIT**] key to escape from the printer control state and start the printout.

11 Wait until the printer finishes printing the first copy, then load your second sheet of paper (as described above) and tap [**EXIT**] again.

12 Take your second copy from the printer.

That is all there is to printing out on your standard settings.

The next few pages examine one of the variations you can make to the standard printing process. Please remember that this Step-by-Step book is not meant to replace your User Instructions Manual. We will *not* be covering every possible eventuality. This book is designed to provide you with a source of *quick* reference, not an alternative source for detailed reference.

■ SECTION 23
Printing a document

In the following pages we will concentrate on covering those variations you are most likely to need in the normal course of your work. For detailed descriptions of every possible variation you can make, please refer to your manual. In the meantime:

1 Try tapping the key labelled **[PTR]** to put the PCW into **printer control mode**. If you look at the bottom line of the Locoscript control area you will see a list of the changes you can make from here. Call up each of the function key menus in turn, have a look at the options and then tap **[CAN]** to cancel the menu. Tap **[EXIT]** when you have finished.

Printing part of a document

Starting from the Disk Management Screen:

1 Move your files cursor onto the file called **PCWINFO1** in Group 1, drive A. Tap **[P]** to print this file.

2 When you see the flag menu, move the highlighting bar down to the 'Print part of document' line (notice that the arrowhead moves down with the bar). Tap **[ENTER]**.

This flag menu tells you the name of the file and it tells you that the first page is numbered "1" and the last page is numbered "3". It is also set to print out from page 1 to page 3 inclusive. We will print page 2 only.

3 Key in the number **[2]** and tap **[ENTER]** to confirm that setting. Move the highlighting bar down one line and key in the number **[2]** again. Tap **[ENTER]** to confirm this setting.

4 Put a sheet of your standard typing paper in the printer — first, check that the printer's **tractor feed** (for continuous stationery) is *not* fitted. (If it is fitted, remove it by unclipping the front edge and then lift and hinge the unit backwards, so that the two hooks at the back of the unit clear their locating holes.) Fit the paper tray.

5 Take a sheet of your typing paper and slip it gently between the casing of the printer and the back surface of the printer platen (the black rubber roller). Line up the left-hand edge of the paper with the third rib on the printer casing.

Towards the right-hand end of the platen you will see two levers. The one to the rear of the platen is the **paper release lever**; the one just in front of the platen is the **paper load lever**.

6 Move the paper load lever towards the front of the printer to its *fullest* extent. This lever has two positions and you should move it through the first 'stop' to the second. Then let it return about a third of the way back to the first 'stop'. The printer will now feed your paper in, leaving it in position ready for you to start printing.

7 If you want to adjust the position of the paper, move the paper release lever towards the front of the printer. This will allow you to move the paper into the right position.

8 When you have finished adjusting your paper, reset the paper release lever *and* the paper load lever.

9 Tap [ENTER] to tell the PCW to proceed.

When you load the printer the PCW assumes that you may want to make a number of adjustments to the printer, so it automatically goes into its **printer control state** (or MODE). If you look at the three bright lines at the top of the screen you will see that they have changed (notice particularly that **PCW9512** is flashing at the left of the second line).

10 For our purposes now, just tap the [EXIT] key to escape from the printer control state and then tap [ENTER] to confirm that you wish to proceed with printing page 2 of the document.

PART THREE

Tailoring page layouts

■ SECTION 25

Changing the margins for the whole text

Starting from the Disk Management Screen:

1 Load the file of your choice (select it at the disk manager menu and then tap **[E]** and **[ENTER]**). Leave your cursor at the start of the file. Hold down a **[SHIFT]** key and tap **[f2/f1]**.

2 We want to change the layout, so move the highlighting bar down one line and tap **[ENTER]**.

Even though the text is still on screen, you cannot change it. If you look closely you will see that the text cursor has disappeared. The cursor in the ruler line – formerly a **ghost cursor** – is now active.

3 To set the **left** margin at character position 5, move the cursor left with the cursor arrow keys until it is on character position 5.

4 Now tap **[f2/f1]**. Make sure that the option 'Set left margin' is highlighted and tap **[ENTER]**.

5 To set the **right** margin at character position 60, move the cursor to character position 60. Tap **[f2/f1]**, highlight the 'Set right margin' option and tap **[ENTER]** and then **[EXIT]** to finish.

6 Hold down a **[SHIFT]** key and tap **[DOC/PAGE]** to reset the whole document to the new margins.

7 Tap **[EXIT]** if you have finished editing.

8 Select the option you want from the EXIT menu and then tap **[ENTER]** to confirm your choice.

Don't forget that if you have saved your document on drive M, you will have to copy it onto one of your floppy disks if you want a permanent copy.

■ SECTION 26

Changing the margins for part of the text

Starting from the Disk Management Screen:

1 Load the file of your choice (select it at the disk manager menu and then tap **[E]** and **[ENTER]**). Move your cursor to the start of the text you want to lay out differently from the rest. Hold down a **[SHIFT]** key and tap **[f2/f1]**.

2 We want the text to be in a new layout, so make sure that this option is highlighted and tap **[ENTER]**.

Even though the text is still on screen, you cannot change it. If you look closely you will see that the text cursor has disappeared. The cursor in the ruler line – formerly a **ghost cursor** – is now active.

3 To set the **left** margin at character position 20, move the cursor to character position 20 on the **ruler line**.

4 Now tap **[f2/f1]**. Make sure that the option 'Set left margin' is highlighted and tap **[ENTER]**.

5 To set the **right** margin at character position 50, move the cursor to character position 50 on the ruler line. Tap **[f2/f1]**, highlight the 'Set right margin' option and tap **[ENTER]**, followed by **[EXIT]** to finish entering the details for your new layout.

You may find that your text seems to have moved across a little. Why?

6 Hold down a **[SHIFT]** key and tap the **[f8/f7]** key. Tap the **[+]** (SET) key and then tap **[ENTER]** to show the state of the (word-processing) codes on the screen.

You will see that the PCW has inserted the code '(LayouT)' into the text.

7 Now move your cursor down to the place in the text where you want this 'new' layout to end.

Changing the margins for part of the text

8 Hold down a **[SHIFT]** key and tap **[f2/f1]**, tap **[ENTER]** to set a new layout, then reset the margins using the same procedure as above. Then tap **[EXIT]** to finish entering this 'new' layout.

9 Move your cursor through the document to reset it to the new margins.

10 Tap **[EXIT]** if you have finished editing.

11 Select the option you want from the EXIT menu and tap **[ENTER]** to confirm your choice.

Don't forget that if you have saved your document on drive M, you will have to copy it onto one of your floppy disks if you want a permanent copy.

■ SECTION 27
Setting tabs

We want to alter the layout by putting in tabs so, starting from the
Disk Management Screen:

1   Hold down a **[SHIFT]** key and tap **[f2/f1]**. Highlight the
option to change the existing layout and then tap **[ENTER]**.

The Locoscript control area changes and the top line reminds you
that you are editing the layout settings. Notice **f3=Tabs** in the
bottom row of the control area.

2   Tap the **[f4/f3]** key. As I don't know if you have any tabs
set, let us begin by making sure that you start with a
clean sheet. Move the bar down the menu to the 'Clear all
Tabs' option.

Before you execute that instruction, notice that you can set four
different types of tab from this menu. However, I want to show
you another quicker way.

3   Tap the **[ENTER]** key to clear your tabs.

Note that you are still editing the layout. Now we can look at the
quick way of setting tabs:

4   Move your ruler line cursor to where you want the first tab
to be — say, on character position 5. Now tap [+], the SET
key, once. A right-pointing arrow appears in the ruler line.
This marks where you have set a normal or **simple tab**.

5   Without moving the cursor, tap the [+] key again. The
right-pointing arrow turns into a left pointing arrow. You
have now put in a **right tab**.

6   Tap [+] once more. The left-pointing arrow changes to one
which points both right and left. This signifies a **centre tab**.

7   Tap [+] one last time. The black blob indicates that a
decimal tab has been set here.

■ **SECTION 27**

Setting tabs

Note:

■ A **simple tab** behaves just like the tab on a typewriter, i.e. the cursor jumps straight to the tab column ready for you to key in text. The text *moves to the right* as you key it in.

■ With a **right tab** the text *moves to the left* as you key it in.

■ With a **centre tab** the text *ranges itself to the right and left of the tab* column as you key it in.

■ The **decimal tab** acts like a combination of a left tab and a right tab.

You would normally use a decimal tab to line up columns of numbers. As you start to key the number in, the individual numbers move to the left *until* you key in a decimal point. They then move to the right.

8 Put in the tabs you want, using the procedure above and, when you have finished, tap the **[EXIT]** key to finish editing the layout and to return to editing your text.

You will see your tab settings in the ruler line.

■ SECTION 28

Indenting text temporarily

When you are creating a document that presents complex information, you will help your readers if you can show which bits of the information are subordinate to others. One of the best ways to do this is to indent the subordinate text. You could do this by changing the margins, but why go through that rigmarole if you want to indent a single paragraph? There is a better way.

Starting from the Disk Management Screen:

1 Load the file of your choice (select it at the disk manager menu and then tap **[E]** and **[ENTER]**).

This procedure assumes that you have tabs set for this document. If you do not, set them now (see Section 27).

2 Move the cursor down to the start of a paragraph that you want to indent. (If you are keying in text and you want to indent the next paragraph, move to the line on which the paragraph will start.)

3 Hold down the **[ALT]** key and tap **[TAB]**.

The symbol on screen (like a tab symbol with a bar on the tail) indicates that a temporary indent has been set here. If you are keying in new text, just go ahead.

If you are working on an existing document:

1 Tap the **[UNIT/PARA]** key and watch the PCW re-lay the paragraph to one tab setting. Now hold down **[ALT]** and this time tap the **[TAB]** key twice.

2 Now tap the **[UNIT/PARA]** key again to re-lay this paragraph, this time to two tab stops.

3 Tap the **[UNIT/PARA]** key once more and you will see that the next paragraph is unaffected.

Thus you can see that indenting text temporarily is really very quick and simple.

Controlling the page length

You need to be able to control the page length for a document in two ways:

■ First, you must be able to end a page and start a new one whenever you want, e.g. when you want to end one section and begin the next on the following page.

■ Secondly, you will want to specify that a certain document will be printed on a particular length of paper, i.e. so many lines per page.

Forcing a page break

The first way is known as **forcing a page break** and may be effected, starting from the Disk Management Screen, as follows:

1 Load the file of your choice (select it at the disk manager menu and then tap **[E]** and **[ENTER]**).

2 Move your cursor down the page until you get to where you want the PCW to start a new page.

3 Hold down **[ALT]** and tap **[RETURN]** – and that is it!

Notice that the PCW has put the broad 'end of page' line across the screen.

Changing the document set-up

The second procedure involves changing the way that the document has been set up.

1 With the document displayed on screen, tap **[f2/f1]**, then select 'Document setup' and tap **[ENTER]**. Look in the Locoscript control area and you will see – on the bottom line – that **f5=Page functions**. Tap **[f6/f5]**.

■ SECTION 29
Controlling the page length

The PCW displays a flag menu with five 'page' options (plus the option to Exit). Explore these on your own later. The one we want now is the one that enables us to select the type of paper which this document will use.

2 Ensure that the 'Paper type' option is highlighted and tap **[ENTER]**.

This flag menu shows you which type of paper is now selected (the one with the tick against it). It tells you whether the printing will be portrait or landscape (the paper lengthways or sideways in the printer) and the bottom section allows you either to use the paper type which has been specified, or take a look at its dimensions.

3 Move the black bar onto one of the paper types that does not have a tick against it and then tap **[+]**, the SET key, to move the tick mark.

4 Tap **[ENTER]** and then **[EXIT]**. Then tap **[ENTER]** again. One more time, tap **[EXIT]**, followed by **[ENTER]** to get back to your editing.

What you have actually done here is to specify that the document you are editing will be printed out on a particular type of paper. The PCW will automatically work out the number of lines on the page if you select one of its standard library of paper types. If you intend to use an unusual paper size, you can enter the details of that paper type into the PCW, to add it to the library. Here you can store the details of 10 different paper types.

(See Session 20 in your Amstrad PCW9512 User Instructions book, around page 243.)

■ SECTION 30
Changing the character and line spacing

From time to time you may want to change the print wheel on your printer and print out with a different spacing, e.g. 12 cpi instead of 10, or you may want to select a different line spacing, e.g. double spaced for a draft manuscript. There are two ways to make such changes. Here is the first; for the second, see the next Section.

Starting from the Disk Management Screen:

1 Load the file of your choice by selecting it at the disk manager menu and then tapping **[E]** and **[ENTER]**.

2 Hold down a **[SHIFT]** key and tap **[f4/f3]**. The flag menu that appears enables you to change a number of different things about the way your document will be printed. The first section is character pitch.

3 Move the highlighting bar down one line. You will see a tick against the current setting. Tap the **[SPACEBAR]** and you will see the menu cursor and the tick jump to the next setting on the right. Keep tapping **[SPACEBAR]** until the tick lands on the setting you want.

Normal width and **Double width** refer to how much space each character will use. On your daisywheel printer a double width character will have extra spacing – t h i s   i s   w h a t I m e a n. On a dot-matrix printer, each character will be literally twice as wide as normal.

4 Move the bar down to the 'line spacing' section – onto the row of numbers. Here also, tapping the **[SPACEBAR]** will move the tick to let you select the setting you want. Choose, say, double spacing, i.e. the number 2.

The 'CR extra spacing' setting determines how much vertical space is entered into the text when you press the **[RETURN]** (Carriage Return) key. We will leave that and the same goes for the Line pitch setting, i.e. how many lines the printer will print per inch, as it is for now.

5 We have specified the changes we want so tap **[ENTER]** to tell the PCW to execute them. Nothing seems to have happened on the screen, so tap **[DOC/PAGE]** and watch as your cursor moves through the text, resetting as it goes.

■ SECTION 31

Using the SET and CLEAR menus

If you have worked through any of the procedures in this Part you will see that you have a great deal of control over the way your document will be laid out on the page. But so far you have seen only one way of achieving the end result you want — by working through a series of flag menus in each procedure. The PCW offers you another, much quicker, way of achieving many of the same results. Bear in mind that the flag menus you have seen, in many cases, are there to provide you with ways of switching Locoscript controls on and off. Put another way, they enable you to SET and CLEAR Locoscript controls. In many instances, the **SET** and **CLEAR** keys offer you an alternative and quicker way of doing the same jobs.

Starting from the Disk Management Screen:

1 Highlight the file **LSINFO** in Group 1, drive A. Tap **[E]** and **[ENTER]** to call that file onto your screen.

2 Now tap [+], the SET key, at the extreme bottom left of the keyboard. Wait for a moment.

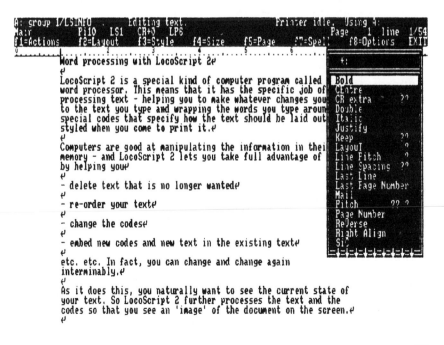

89

■ SECTION 31

Using the SET and CLEAR menus

The cursor disappears from the text and at the same time a long flag menu unfurls from the top of the ruler line. This is the **SET menu**. If you look at the bottom of the menu you will see a row of arrows which tells you that there are more options on offer. Notice that, at the moment, the bottom line of the menu reads 'SiC'.

3 Hold down a [SHIFT] key and tap the [↓].

The bottom line of the menu now reads '-hard hyphen'; the previous bottom line (SiC) is now about a third of the way up. Notice also that there is now a row of arrows at the top of the menu.

4 Hold down a [SHIFT] key and tap [↑] to move back to the top of the menu. Move the black bar down a line, onto the 'CEntre' option (remember your **text cursor** was on the top line of the text).

5 Keep an eye on the top line of the text and tap [ENTER]. The top line of text will jump to the centre of the page as the menu disappears from the screen. That was because you had selected 'CEntre' from the SET menu.

6 Tap [←DEL] and watch what happens.

The text returns to its previous position because you have deleted the Locoscript control code that caused the text to be centred. So remember – **it is usually possible to cancel the effect of a control code by simply deleting the code itself**.

7 In a moment I want you to key in the following sequence of keys as quickly as you can. Tap [+] [C] [E] [ENTER] and then look at the top line of your text.

You have achieved exactly the same end result as you did by working through the menu. This means that, once you have got used to the various codes, the **SET** key provides you with a very quick way of controlling and enhancing your text (see also the remainder of this Part, as well as Part 4).

Using the SET and CLEAR menus

8 Tap the [+] key and have a good look at the menu. The key letters for the various codes are the ones in capitals. That's how the PCW differentiates between codes which start with the same letter. For example, to change the **L**ine **S**pacing to **2**, key in **[L] [S] [2]**.

9 Tap the **CLEAR** key, marked [−] (next to the SET key). Again, wait for a moment.

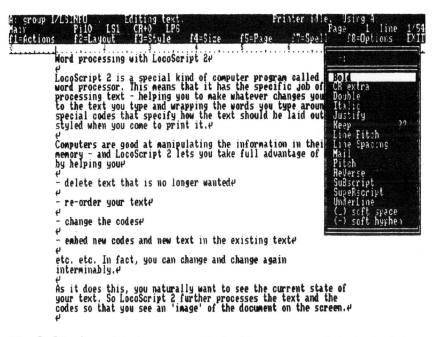

The [+] key enabled you to switch things on, so it is logical that the [−] key should switch them off again. Why, then, is the **CLEAR menu** so much shorter than the **SET menu**?

If you think about it the answer is simple. First, some of the controls on the SET menu, such as the CEntre option, operate for one line only. With others − like LayouT, for example − you switch off by switching another LayouT on. Yet others, are 'global' commands, which are used only once in a document, e.g. Last Page Number. Those facts whittle down the list to the one you have on screen now.

Using the SET and CLEAR menus

The key point remains though: you use the [+] key to **SET** certain attributes ON, and you use the [−] key to **CLEAR** certain settings from the text!

10 Tap the [CAN] key and then [EXIT] to abandon this file, leaving the original unchanged.

■ SECTION 32
Justifying text to both margins

If you want a really professional looking finish to your text then one of the devices you can adopt is **right-justification** – making the right-hand ends of lines of text line up with the right margin. The text you are reading now is right-justified.

This paragraph, on the other hand, is not right-justified – it has a 'ragged' right edge. You need to make up your own mind about which looks best, but it is generally held that justified text looks better – probably because it is hard to do with a typewriter. Some experiments have shown that justified text is marginally (ho, ho!) more difficult to read.

Here is how you would justify your text. There are three methods.

First method

Starting from the Disk Management Screen:

1 Highlight the file **LSINFO** in Group 1 on drive A. Tap **[E]** and **[ENTER]** to call that file onto your screen. At the moment the text in this file is **un**justified. We will justify it to see how it looks.

2 Hold down a **[SHIFT]** key and tap **[f2/f1]**. Move the black bar to the 'Change layout' option and tap **[ENTER]**.

The Locoscript control area reminds you that you are editing a layout. Look at the bottom line of the control area see the actions you can carry out now.

3 Hold down a **[SHIFT]** key and tap the **[f8/f7]** key.

The first option on this flag menu is concerned with justification. At the moment there is no tick against it which means that it has not been set on.

4 Tap the **[SPACEBAR]** once and the tick appears. Tap **[SPACEBAR]** again and it goes again. So the **[SPACEBAR]** acts like a **toggle** switch. Tap **[SPACEBAR]** once more to turn justification on. Then tap **[ENTER]** followed by **[EXIT]** to get back to the text editing mode.

■ SECTION 32
Justifying text to both margins

You can use the **[SPACEBAR]** as a toggle on many of the PCW's flag menus.

Nothing has happened to your text yet. It still has a ragged right edge.

5 Hold down a **[SHIFT]** key, tap the **[DOC/PAGE]** key and watch the change ripple through the text.

Second method

Now for the second way of altering the justification setting. Let us assume for the moment that you want all of the text justified except for the last but one paragraph. Here's how to do it. Remember that at the moment justification is ON for the whole document.

1 Hold down the **[ALT]** key and tap **[UNIT/PARA]** twice. (Remember that the **[ALT]** key reverses the action of most of the special cursor keys.)

2 Your cursor should be somewhere around line 44 on page 1 of the file − at the start of the paragraph beginning 'LocoScript 2 also organises...'.

3 Tap [−], the CLEAR key, followed by **[J]** to turn justification OFF at this point in the text. Now tap the **[UNIT/PARA]** key and watch the paragraph reset to a ragged right edge.

4 With your cursor at the start of the last paragraph, turn justification back ON again. Tap [+], the SET key, followed by **[J]**.

Third method

The third way of switching justification on and off is also very easy, but you need to be aware of the effects of the justification codes you have put into the text. However, before we start:

■ SECTION 32
Justifying text to both margins

1 Hold down a **[SHIFT]** key and tap the **[f8/f7]** key. Tap the **[SPACEBAR]** to toggle the codes display on and then tap **[ENTER]**. Now you will be able to see the codes you have just put in.

2 Hold down a **[SHIFT]** key and tap the **[f2/f1]** key.

Notice that this is also the first step in the first method I described above. The bottom line of this menu says **Clear justification**. So the PCW 'knows' that justification has been set on.

3 Tap the **[CAN]** key to cancel the menu without changing the settings. Move the cursor to the start of the text: **[ALT]** **[SHIFT]** and **[DOC/PAGE]**.

4 Hold down a **[SHIFT]** key and tap **[f2/f1]** again.

5 Move the bar down the menu to the 'Clear justification' option and tap **[ENTER]**. The PCW puts a code into your text.

6 Now hold down **[SHIFT]** and tap **[DOC/PAGE]** and watch what happens.

Now all of the text is **un**justified except for the last paragraph. The last paragraph is still justified because you have the code (+Just) at the start of the paragraph which switched the justification back on again.

So you can turn justification on and off in three ways. Remember that in methods 2 and 3 you have put codes into the text that affected subsequent justification commands.

7 Tap **[EXIT]** and **[A]** followed by **[ENTER]** to abandon this file, leaving the original unchanged.

■ SECTION 33
Centring and right-aligning lines

In this section we are going to look at how you can position single lines of text across the page. The natural position of a line of text is with its first character level with the left margin. In typographic jargon, normal text is **ranged left**. But you can also **range** the text about the **centre** of the page and you can **range** it to the **right**. As usual with the PCW, there are various ways of positioning the text.

Centring text

Starting from the Disk Management Screen:

1 Highlight the file **POEM.EG** in Group 1 in drive A. Tap [**E**] and [**ENTER**] to call that file onto your screen.

2 Hold down a [**SHIFT**] key and then tap [**f2/f1**].

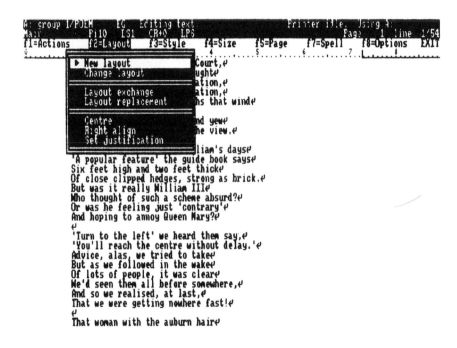

Centring and right-aligning lines

At the bottom of this 'layout flag menu' you will see three options. The last one – Set justification – allows you to control the text in the whole document. The other two control the position of single lines and these are the ones that concern us here.

3 Move the highlighting bar down the menu to the 'Centre' option. Keep your eye on the first line of the poem and tap **[ENTER]**. Everything **to the right of the cursor** is spread evenly about the centre line of the page.

4 Now hold down a **[SHIFT]** key and tap the **[LINE/EOL]** key, to move the cursor to the start of the next line. We will centre this line too, but by a different method.

5 In quick succession, tap **[+]**, **[C]** and then **[E]** to centre the second line of text.

6 Keep repeating that same procedure and reset the whole of the first verse to the centre: **[SHIFT] [LINE/EOL]** then **[+] [C] [E]**.

```
A: group 1/POEM    LG  Editing text.              Printer idle.  Using A:
Main       Pi10  LS1  CR+0  LP6                      Page    1 line  9/54
f1=Actions   f2=Layout   f3=Style   f4=Size   f5=Page   f7=Spell   f8=Options   EXIT
                     Once on a visit to Hampton Court,↵
                     Someone suggested that we ought↵
                     To prove our skill in navigation,↵
                     Attempt with careful observation,↵
                  To follow the intricate paths that wind↵
                     In and out and on behind↵
                  Tall hedges made of thorn and yew↵
                  Which everywhere do block the view.↵

        The Maze was planted in William's days↵
        'A popular feature' the guide book says↵
        Six feet high and two feet thick↵
        Of close clipped hedges, strong as brick.↵
        But was it really William III↵
        Who thought of such a scheme absurd?↵
        Or was he feeling just 'contrary'↵
        And hoping to annoy Queen Mary?↵
        ↵
        'Turn to the left' we heard them say,↵
        'You'll reach the centre without delay.'↵
        Advice, alas, we tried to take↵
        But as we followed in the wake↵
        Of lots of people, it was clear↵
        We'd seen them all before somewhere,↵
        And so we realised, at last,↵
        That we were getting nowhere fast!↵
        ↵
        That woman with the auburn hair↵
```

Centring and right-aligning lines

So you have seen two ways of centring the text between the margins. Use the one which suits you best. My own preference is the SET key method, because I find it quicker, but perhaps you are not in such a hurry as I am.

Aligning a single line

Next, we will look at aligning a single line of text with the right margin, i.e. ranging right. The procedures are very similar. The first method is as follows:

1   Move your cursor to the start of the second verse. Hold down a **[SHIFT]** key and tap **[f2/f1]**.

2   Move the highlighting bar down the menu to the 'Right align' option and tap **[ENTER]**. This time everything to the right of the cursor moves right across the page so that the last character in the line is level with the right margin.

Now, again, for our second method of right-aligning the text:

1   Hold down a **[SHIFT]** key and tap **[LINE/EOL]** to get to the start of the next line.

2   Now tap [+] followed by **[R] [A]**.

3   Again, keep repeating the procedure to reset the rest of this verse: (**[SHIFT]** and **[LINE/EOL]**, then [+] **[R] [A]**).

■ SECTION 33

Centring and right-aligning lines

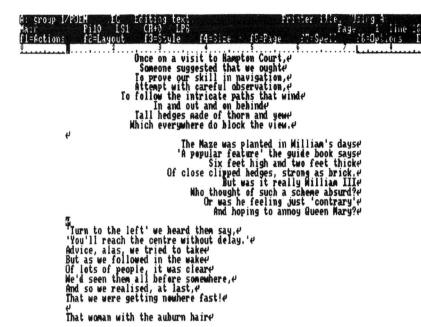

Here also, choose the method you prefer. I think you will agree that neither of them is difficult.

■ **SECTION 34**

Creating a new standard template

You will know that Locoscript divides up the storage space on a disk into eight 'compartments' and that it deals with those compartments as if they held eight different groupings of files. Start up Locoscript, go to the Disk Management Screen and you will see what I mean.

```
                  Disc management.                Printer file.  Using none.
C=Create new document       E=Edit document       P=Print document      D=Direct printing
f1=Actions  f2=Disc  f3=File  f4=Group  f5=Document  f6=Settings  f7=Disc change f8=Options
Drive A:                   Drive B:        not fitted Drive M:
173k used   0k free  12 files  0k used  0k free  0 files  2k used  60k free   2 files

   group 0  173k     group 4   0k                        group 0   2k     group 4   0k
   group 1    0k     group 5   0k                        group 1   0k     group 5   0k
   group 2    0k     group 6   0k                        group 2   0k     group 6   0k
   group 3    0k     group 7   0k                        group 3   0k     group 7   0k
 A: group 0    12 files M: group 0    2 files
    0 limbo files       0 limbo files
 LOCOCHAR.2     25k
 LOCOCHAR.3      8k      2 hidden     2k
 LOCOCHAR.BAS   14k
 LOCOCHAR.KEY    1k
 PHRASES .STD    1k
 READ    .ME     6k
 SETTINGS.STD    1k
    5 hidden   117k
```

Scan through the list of files in each group and you will see that most of the groups contain a file called **TEMPLATE.STD** (in fact, the majority contain nothing else). Although they all have the same name, they are different files — one for each group. So why are they there? To answer that question you will have to think about the procedures you go through when you create a new document. Before you start keying in text you will have to have an idea of the tabs you may require, how wide the text should be on the page, whether you want headers and/or footers, and what size paper you want the document to be printed on. Potentially there are many more things you might wish to specify.

100

Creating a new standard template

If you had to specify all the features of the document each time you started a new file, I'm sure you would find that unacceptable. So the PCW provides you with three options:

■ In default of any instructions from you, Locoscript will set up certain basic features for the new document − based on the assumption that you will be using a certain size of paper and that you will be printing the document with the PCW's own printer. (These are known as the **default settings**.)

■ You can (if you want to) tailor these default settings for **an individual document** − for example, by putting in special tabs, or adding headers or footers. But then you will have to remember these settings for the next time you decide to create a similar document.

■ You can set up a standard pattern or template for each **TYPE** of document you may create, then store that template in a compartment on the disk (a group) which is set aside for that one TYPE of document.

It is the third option that concerns us here, because that is the function of those files you can see called TEMPLATE.STD. So how do you set up a template of your own design?

The actual process of setting up a standard template file is very straightforward. You create it (under the name TEMPLATE.STD) just as you would create any other document − and we will see that in a moment. As for the template itself − in other words the **CONTENTS** of the template file − well you can make that as complicated or as simple as you like. Your PCW9512 User Instruction Book (in Session 24) takes you through a very detailed explanation of just what is possible, but in this section I want to concentrate on the sort of settings the average person is likely to use for the majority of his or her work.

1 Move your groups cursor Group 1 on drive A and then tap [C] to create a new document.

2 Key in the file name TEMPLATE.STD and tap **[ENTER]** to open the file and get the blank page display on screen.

■ SECTION 34
Creating a new standard template

Had there already been a file called TEMPLATE.STD in this group the PCW would have displayed an **error flag** giving you the chance to choose another name for the file, replace the existing file with the one you are about to create, or abandoning the activity.

Because Group 1 does not contain a 'template' file, the page display you have now is the one that embodies the PCW's default settings. Let us set up a template that is going to be of practical use in the future — we will create a template for your letters.

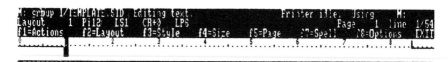

What are the design criteria?:

■ We will use the most popular paper size, e.g. A4 in Europe.

■ We may need to use tabs.

■ The standard template should include your address.

■ We want the text to be easy to read, so it should not be wider than 5.5 inches and it should be unjustified.

■ We do not want the pages numbered.

■ We will use the PCW's own printer, printing at 10 characters per inch (cpi).

So let's set up the template to meet these criteria:

1 First, tabs and margins (in other words 'layout'). Hold down a **[SHIFT]** key and tap the **[f2/f1]** key. Select 'change layout' and tap **[ENTER]**.

2 The left margin is set at 10, which is fine, so move the ruler line cursor to character position 65 (so the text will be 55 characters wide, or 5.5 inches at 10 cpi).

3 Tap the **[f2/f1]** key, select 'Set right margin' with ↓ and tap **[ENTER]**.

Creating a new standard template

4 Now tabs. Three will usually be enough. Move the ruler line cursor to character position 15 (half an inch in from the margin) and then tap **[f4/f3]**. A simple tab will do, so just tap **[ENTER]**. Do the same at character positions 20 and 25. Finally, tap **[EXIT]** to get back to editing mode.

5 Now let us just check that the other criteria are set as we want them. Hold down a **[SHIFT]** key and tap **[f1/f2]**.

The bottom line on that flag menu tells us that (right) justification is *not* set on at the moment, so that is okay.

6 Tap the **[CAN]** key and then hold down a **[SHIFT]** key and tap **[f4/f3]**. Here we can see that the printer settings are also as we want them. (Notice, the character pitch is 10.)

7 Tap the **[CAN]** key. And now for your address.

You will want to select your own style for the address, but for this exercise I'm assuming that you want your name in double width with the address in normal width text. I'm also assuming that the whole thing will be printed in a bold typeface.

8 As we will be putting in some print control codes, it will be helpful if we can see them, so hold down a **[SHIFT]** key and tap **[f8/f7]**. Now tap [+] and **[ENTER]**.

9 Tap [+], followed by **[B]** (for bold print), and now [+] and **[P]** for pitch, key in the number **10** and then **[D]** for double width (*not* double strike). Remember that when you print with the PCW's own printer, double width actually means double spacing between the characters.

10 Now key in your own name, but *don't* press **[RETURN]** when you have finished, because we want the rest of the text to be in normal width characters. Instead, tap [−], followed by **[P]** to switch the pitch change off. Then tap **[RETURN]**. Now key in your address, one line at a time. Do not press **[RETURN]** on the last line.

Creating a new standard template

11 Remember that we set bold printing on at the start of this text, so now let us switch it off again. Tap [−] and then [B], followed by [RETURN].

So there is your name and address lined up with the left margin, but it is likely that you would prefer it either in the centre of the page, or aligned to the right.

12 Move the cursor up to the last line of the address and then tap [+], followed by [C] [E] to centre it or [R] [A] to right-align it. Repeat the process for the complete name and address block.

You can see the text *and* the control codes you have inserted. If in future you don't want the codes on screen, remember to clear the setting now..! ([SHIFT], [f8/f7], [−], [ENTER]). Remember that your name is set in double width characters, which explains the odd looking layout. Tap the [DOC/PAGE] key to tidy up.

Unless you want to make any further changes of your own, that's all there is to creating our new template. So:

1 Tap [EXIT] and then [ENTER] to save a copy of the file in group 1 on the disk in drive A.

2 But you probably will not want this template in group 1 so let us MOVE it into the letters group. Make sure that the files cursor is on TEMPLATE.STD in group 1 and then tap the [f4/f3] key. Highlight the 'Move file' option and tap [ENTER]. Now move the files cursor one column to the right and tap [ENTER].

3 Tap [ENTER] again to confirm your actions and after a short pause you will see an error flag.

■ SECTION 34
Creating a new standard template

M: group 1/TEMPLATE.STD Moving file.   Printer idle. Using   M:
f1=Actions f2=Disc f3=File f4=Group f5=Document f6=Settings f7=Disc change f8=Options
Drive A: Drive B: not fitted Drive M:
173k used   0k free 12 files 0k used   0k free 0 files 3k used   59k free   3 files

  group 0 173k   group 4   0k   group 0   2k   group 4   0k
  group 1   0k   group 5   0k   group 1   1k   group 5   0k
  group 2   0k   group 6   0k   group 2   0k   group 6   0k
  group 3   0k   group 7   0k   group 3   0k   group 7   0k

A: group 0   12 files M:┌──ERROR in: Move file──────────────┐s
   0 limbo files   │   │
LOCOCHAR.2   25k   │ Filenames must be different   │
LOCOCHAR.3   8k   │ ► Choose another name   │
LOCOCHAR.BAS 14k   │   Cancel operation   │
LOCOCHAR.KEY   1k   └─────────────────────────────────────┘
PHRASES .STD   1k
READ   .ME   6k
SETTINGS.STD   1k
   5 hidden 117k

The problem is that you cannot have two files with the same name in the same group, so you can either 'cancel the operation' or you can choose another name for your file. However, if you do the latter, it won't work as a template file — it *must* be called TEMPLATE.STD. You can, however, replace the existing file with this one. That is what we must do, and that option is highlighted, so:

1 Tap **[ENTER]** and wait for the display to update itself.

2 With your cursor still in the LETTERS group, tap **[C]** and **[ENTER]** to create a new file. And there you are with a working template.

3 Tap **[DOC/PAGE]** and then key in some experimental text. When you have finished, save and print your 'letter'.

4 Don't forget to erase the test document when you have read the print out.

105

■ SECTION 34
Creating a new standard template

So now you have seen that the actual procedure for creating a new template file is not difficult or complicated. It is really just like creating any other kind of document.

But remember that if you want the file to work as a standard template for documents within a certain group, then the file must be called TEMPLATE.STD and it must be stored in the group in question.

PART FOUR

Enhancing the printed page

■ SECTION 35
Printing words underlined

Starting from the Disk Management Screen:

1 Move your files cursor onto the file called **diskINFO** in the group 1 column. Tap **[E]** and then **[ENTER]** to edit this document.

2 Tap the **[UNIT/PARA]** key to move to the start of the second paragraph. Now tap [+] followed by **[U]** and **[L]**. Nothing seems to happen, but...

3 Move the cursor to the right until it is in the space between the word **easy** and the word **to**. Now tap the [−] followed by **[U][L]** and watch what happens.

4 Tap **[UNIT/PARA]** again, followed by **[+][U][L]** and then **[DOC/PAGE]**. Again, watch your screen.

5 Turn the underline function off again with the combination of keys you used before: [−]**[U][L]**.

```
A: group 1/DISCINFO.     Editing text.          Printer idle.  Using 4
Main        File   LS1   CR+0   LP6                         Page   2  Line 1/54
f1=Actions  f2=Layout  f3=Style   f4=Size   f5=Page   f7=Spell  f8=Options  EXIT
0.........1.........2.........3.........4.........5.........6.........7.........L.........
```

```
        ┙
        - how to produce copies of documents┙
        ┙
        - how to get rid of documents you no longer need┙
        ┙
        - how to give discs, groups and documents names, and┙
        ┙
        - how to set up and inspect a short description of a document┙
        ┙
        These are the basic tools that enable you to keep your disks
        organised.┙
        ┙
        We shall also show you how to make back-up copies of your more
        important discs - to keep in case of accidents, like someone
        spilling coffee over the disk or repeatedly leaving it in the
        drive while switching your PCW on or off. Discretion is the
        better part of valour!┙
        ┙
        Every operation is carried out on the Disk Manager Screen -
        that is, the screen on which the names of your documents are
        displayed. ┙
        ┙
```

```
        For most of the operations, we will be using the three Disk
        Manager menus called Disc, Files and Group. The Disk menu for
        all the operations involving the whole disk; the Group menu for
        operations on a whole group; and the Files menu for operations
        on individual documents. As always, the keys that you need to
```

■ SECTION 35
Printing words underlined

So, while you are editing existing text you can add underlining with the method you have seen. But can you key in text which will be automatically underlined?

6 Hold down a **[SHIFT]** key and tap **[DOC/PAGE]**. Tap **[RETURN]** a couple of times so you are clear of the end of the text.

7 Now tap [+][U][L] and then key in **now is the time for all good men**.... Notice that all the letters *and* all the spaces *and* all the punctuation marks are underlined.

8 Now, tap [−][U][L] to switch this form of underlining off again. We can now try something slightly different. Tap [+] and **[W]** and then complete the sentence by keying in **to come to the aid of bad women**.... This time all the letters and all the punctuation marks are underlined, *but* the spaces are not.

This form of underlining is called **word underline** — that's why you tapped [+][W] instead of [+][U][L]. So don't forget that you can call on two types of underlining.

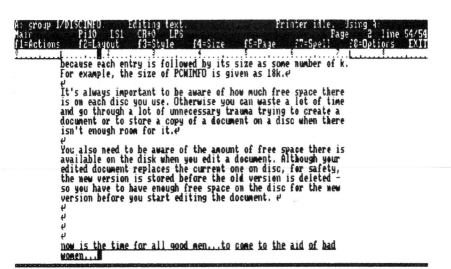

Printing words underlined

As with many of Locoscript's features, you can set them and clear them in two ways – either via the **SET** and **CLEAR** key menus, or by using one of the **function keys**.

9 Tap the **[f4/f3]** key and watch the screen. You will see a flag menu which allows you to set or clear eight different **print attributes** (as they are sometimes known). But you should find that using the **[+]** key is quicker in most instances – except perhaps if you want to set, say a heading, to be underlined *and* bold, in which case, using this menu may be quicker.

10 Tap the **[CAN]** key to get rid of the menu and then abandon the file in memory by tapping **[EXIT]** then **[A]** followed by **[ENTER]**.

The disk copy of the file will be unchanged.

■ SECTION 36
Printing words in bold type

1 Switch your machine on and start up with a copy of your LOCOSCRIPT 2 master disk. Wait until the PCW displays the Disk Management Screen.

2 Move your files cursor onto the file called LSINFO in the group 1 column. Tap **[f4/f3]** followed by **[ENTER]** to copy this file. Move your groups cursor to the "group 1" group on drive M: and tap **[ENTER]** twice to make the copy.

3 Tap **[E]** then **[ENTER]** to edit this document.

■ You can **"embolden"** parts of your text to make them stand out from the rest. You have a choice between **BOLD** type – where each character is printed several times in the same place or **DOUBLE STRIKE** – which, as the name suggests is the same as bold except the character is struck only twice and it therefore does not create such a dark image.

■ As with other "print attributes" you can set bold and double strike printing on/off in two ways: either through the **f3 "style"** menu, or with the **SET** and **CLEAR** keys. For example:

Tap the **[f4/f3]** key.

■ The third and fourth items on the flag menu are "Bold" and "Double strike" respectively, which tells you that you can set them on or off from here.

■ The quicker way to set bold or double strike on and off is with the [+] and [−] keys. Like this:

1 Tap the **[CAN]** key to get rid of the "style" menu. Before we start, let us set the PCW so it shows the print control codes. Hold down a **[SHIFT]** key and tap the **[f8/f7]** key. Tap the [+] (SET) key to put a tick against the "show codes" option and then tap **[ENTER]**.

■ You won't see any changes on screen because we have not yet put any control codes in.

Printing words in bold type

2 Tap [+] followed by the letter [B] (for bold). Now tap **[LINE/ EOL]** to move your cursor to the end of the line, tap [−] [B] to clear the bold setting and you will see the codes added to the text.

■ So now the heading will be printed in a bold typeface. What about double strike? Well it is the same procedure, except that you use [+] [D] instead of [+] [B]. What I want you to do now is to work through the complete file and put in the control codes to set the name "LocoScript 2" to be printed in double strike. We will use another PCW tool to make the job easier.

1 First, hold down the **[ALT]** key and tap **[DOC/PAGE]** to get back to the start of the text.

2 Tap the **[EXCH/FIND]** key. When you see the flag menu, key in LocoScript 2 exactly as it appears here. When you have done that tap **[ENTER]** and watch the screen. The cursor jumps immediately to the first occurrence − in the title (which is already set in bold).

■ Yes you *can* use "double strike" and "bold" in combination to get an even darker image on the page. So:

3 Tap [+] and [D] to set double strike on. Now move the cursor onto the opening bracket immediately AFTER the number 2 and key in [−] (CLEAR) [D].

4 Tap **[EXCH/FIND]** and tap **[ENTER]** to find the next occurrence and again set double strike on and then off again.

■ **Remember...the OFF command goes AFTER the 2!**

5 Repeat the "FIND" and then the "double strike" on/off sequence for the rest of the file.

■ You may have found that a pretty tiresome process, but think how much longer it would have taken − and how easy it is to miss an occurrence − without the FIND facility. So here's a good example of how you can use a combination of tools to make your work easier, yet more thorough.

■ SECTION 36
Printing words in bold type

1 Let's look at the text without the control codes. Hold down a [SHIFT] key and tap [f8/f7]. Tap the [−] (CLEAR) key and tap [ENTER].

2 If you want to see how this looks when it is printed out, tap [EXIT], select the Save and Print option and then tap [ENTER]. If you do not need to see a printed copy, tap [EXIT] [A] and [ENTER].

■ You don't need a permanent copy of the file.

■ SECTION 37
Changing a print wheel

In this section we will simply be looking at how you swap the print wheel on the PCW's own printer. If you are using a different make of "daisy printer" the procedures will not be exactly the same — though they might be similar. I am assuming that your system is switched on and that you have started up with LOCOSCRIPT.

Note   When you change a print wheel and when you want to use a different printer you **MUST** make the relevant adjustments to the PCW's printer settings the **(f6)** menu from the disk manager screen. For detailed instructions, see your PCW9512 User Instructions book, session 23, page 273.

1   Look at the top of your printer. Toward the front edge you will see a translucent grey plastic lid or dust cover. The dust cover is hinged. Hinge this cover up and then down again — to reset the position of the print mechanism.

2   Now hinge the dust cover up to the vertical position and lift it clear of the printer so you have clear access to the innards of the printer.

3   You need to get at the mechanism below the ribbon cartridge, so the next step is to remove the cartridge. Grip the cartridge by the two prongs which point away from you — note where the ribbon itself runs.

4   Gently tilt the cartridge upward — you will feel it click clear of a retaining clip — then lift the cartridge clear of the printer and put it to one side.

5   The print wheel is locked in position, so the first thing to do is to unlock it. Looking down on the mechanism you will see, on the left hand side, a black plastic coated lever. Pull that lever toward you to unlock the print wheel.

6   You will see the print wheel loosen as you unlock it. Now simply lift the printwheel upward — holding it gently by the "petals".

7 Now take your replacement print wheel and holding it between the finger and thumb of one hand by the petals – with the characters facing toward the printer roller – lower it gently into position, just in front of the two ribbon guide lugs.

8 Release the print wheel and it should slip down into the correct position. You do not have to line it up in any special way.

9 Now lock the new wheel into position by pushing the black plastic coated lever toward the printer roller – you will feel and see the lever taking up the slack and then lock into position.

10 Take the ribbon cartridge, with the ribbon end away from you and with the ribbon tensioner to the top. If you look at the end nearest you, you will see two small lugs. Those lugs fit into two slots in the ribbon cartridge carrier on the printer.

11 Slip the cartridge into position, making sure the lugs are located properly, and then apply gentle but firm pressure to the top of the cartridge until you feel it click into place firmly. Check that the ribbon itself runs between the print wheel and the printer roller.

12 Take the dust cover lid and, holding it vertically, slip the right hand end over the hinge and then the left. Finally, close the dust cover.

■ SECTION 38
Changing a ribbon cartridge

1 Look at the top of your printer. Toward the front edge you will see a translucent grey plastic lid or dust cover. The dust cover is hinged.

2 Hinge this cover up to the vertical position and lift it clear of the printer so you have clear access to the innards of the printer.

3 The next step is to remove the old cartridge. Grip the cartridge by the two prongs which point away from you – note where the ribbon itself runs.

4 Gently tilt the cartridge upward – you will feel it click clear of a retaining clip – then lift the cartridge clear of the printer and put it to one side.

5 Take your replacement cartridge with the ribbon end away from you and with the ribbon tensioner to the top.

6 If you look at the end nearest you, you will see two small lugs. Those lugs fit into two slots in the ribbon cartridge carrier on the printer.

7 Slip the cartridge into position, making sure that the lugs are located properly.

8 Then apply gentle but firm pressure to the top of the cartridge until you feel it click firmly into place.

9 Check that the ribbon itself runs between the print wheel and the printer roller.

10 Take the dust cover lid and, holding it vertically, slip the right hand end over the hinge.

11 Then click the left hand end downward into position.

12 Finally, close the dust cover.

■ SECTION 39
Paper sizes and types

When you create a document with your PCW it has to make certain assumptions about the paper you will be printing on – if it didn't know the width of the paper, how would it "know" where to set the margins? If it didn't know the length of the paper, how would it know when to start a new page?

The PCW has been set up to work with a standard size of paper which it will use in default of any instructions from you to do otherwise. How then do you instruct it to use a different size of paper for a particular document?

1 Switch your machine on and start up with a copy of your LOCOSCRIPT 2 master disk. Wait until the PCW displays the Disk Management Screen.

2 Move your files cursor to highlight the file name "DISCINFO" in the group 1 column on disk A: and Tap **[E]** and **[ENTER]** to edit this file.

■ Look at the top of your screen and make a note of the number of lines per page – 54 in Europe with A4 paper. Also notice the margin settings – 10 and 72 in Europe. On A4 paper this document ends at line 50 of 54 on page 2.

■ Paper size is one of the items specified in the set-up details for this (and every other) LOCOSCRIPT file. So let us change it to see the effect.

3 Tap the **[f2/f1]** key. Make sure that "Document setup" is highlighted and tap **[ENTER]**.

■ The PCW is now in "document setup mode". As you can see on screen this is where you can set headers and footers as well as various other features – look in the bottom row of the LOCOSCRIPT control area.

4 Tap the **[f6/f5]** key to gain access to the "page" options. Make sure that "Paper type" is highlighted on the flag menu and then tap **[ENTER]**.

■ SECTION 39
Paper sizes and types

■ This flag menu shows you the paper types which the PCW "knows" about. The one which has been selected for this document has a tick mark against it. (In Europe this will be A4).

5 Move the highlighting bar to another – smaller – paper setting (in Europe, select A5) and tap the [+] (SET) key. Watch the tick mark. Then tap [ENTER].

6 We don't need to alter anything else now, so tap [EXIT] and then [ENTER]. You are still in Document setup mode, so tap [EXIT] and [ENTER] again to get back to where we were.

■ Notice that the margins are the same, but the page length has changed. In Europe, the cursor is now on line 1 of 34.

7 Hold down a [SHIFT] key and tap the [DOC/PAGE] key, to move the cursor to the end of the document. If you move the cursor up one line, you will see that you are on line 34 of 34 on page 3!

■ So changing the paper type has automatically caused the PCW to compensate by changing the page length. Let us set the paper type back to what it was.

8 Tap [f2/f1] and tap [ENTER]. When the display settles down, tap [f6/f5] and tap [ENTER]. Make sure the high-lighting bar is on the PREVIOUS paper selection, then tap [+] (SET) and [ENTER].

Paper sizes and types

■ While we are at this flag menu let us have a look at one of the other items.

9 Move the highlighting bar onto the Page layout option and tap **[ENTER]**.

■ This flag gives you a detailed description of the various "zones" which have been set up for this page. The numbers on the right refer to the number of lines set aside for each zone. Remember that the standard line setting is 6 lines to the vertical inch of paper.

10 Tap **[ENTER]**, then **[EXIT]**, then **[ENTER]** followed by **[EXIT]** **[ENTER]** again to get back to the document.

■ Notice that this time the PCW processes only two pages and the cursor is on line 49 of 54 on page 2. (Remember, you moved it up one line from the bottom just now).

11 Tap **[EXIT] [A]** and **[ENTER]** to abandon this document.

■ The PCW recognises a reasonable selection of paper types and sizes. If you have the need to use a special size of paper – one which the PCW does not recognise – you can add the details of the paper to the PCW's list. See session 20 in your PCW9512 User Instructions Book.

Using other printers with Locoscript 2

Although the PCW's ability to use virtually any type of printer is a valuable feature, I suspect that the "typical" user will be quite happy to work with the printer which comes with the machine. Therefore, as this book is aimed at the typical first-time user, I will not be covering any of the technicalities associated with using other printers. But, having said that, you might well be considering using another printer − if only out of curiosity so I do want to discuss some of the things you will have to bear in mind.

Why would you want to use another printer?   There would seem to be two main possibilities: Firstly you might want a faster printer; or secondly you might want access to a wider range of type faces and "print enhancement" options.

What types of printer are available?   For typical word processing work there are two main types: The **Daisy Wheel Printer** − such as the one which comes with the machine, and the **Dot Matrix Printer**. There are other types of printers, such as Ink Jet, Thimble, Line or Laser, but at the time of writing these are less widely used than the two main ones I have mentioned.

What are the differences between the two main types of printer?   The **daisy wheel** printer has at its "business end" a print wheel which has letters at the end of thin flat "spokes" which radiate from the centre of the wheel like daisy petals (hence the name "daisy wheel").

The printer prints a letter on the paper by moving the appropriate petal into the right position and then striking the back of the petal with a print "hammer". The letter moves forward against the ribbon and then against the paper, so producing a letter on the page. In essence the printing method is the same as an ordinary typewriter.

You get different styles of print by changing the print wheel − each type of print wheel having a different type face, and that's something you can't do with an ordinary typewriter!

The **dot matrix** printer prints in a different way. Instead of having a fixed selection of characters ranged around a wheel which are then struck by a single hammer, the "print head" itself is formed of a bundle of thin rods which can all be moved independently.

In effect, each rod works like a print hammer which strikes the ribbon, creating a printed dot on the paper. When several rods move forward at the same time they create a pattern of dots on the paper – and if you move the right pattern of rods forward at the same time, they create the shape of a letter.

Why would you use one type of printer rather than another? A **daisy wheel** printer generally produces much better quality print...the image is crisp and clean because the shapes of the characters are formed by lines and curves. In fact daisy wheel output is often referred to as **letter quality** printing.

But the printing mechanism has to work very hard to achieve high printing speeds. A rating of 50 characters per second (50 cps) is a good one for a daisy wheel printer. But speed ratings can be misleading. Often the speed rating given for a printer is actually its maximum speed. A printer with a maximum speed of 50cps is likely to have an average printing speed of somewhere between 30 and 40 cps. So, if QUALITY of output is paramount, then you would probably want to use some kind of daisy wheel printer with a single strike ribbon (that is a ribbon which can be used just once).

If, however, speed is more important than quality, (for producing drafts, for example) then you would do better to opt for a dot matrix printer. In fact, some of the modern printers can produce a pretty acceptable finish – **Near Letter Quality** or **NLQ** as it is known.

Generally speaking, because the dot matrix printer forms the outline of a character with dots rather than lines and curves, the quality of output cannot be as crisp and clean as the daisy wheel (that's why the best output is called NEAR letter quality rather than letter quality).

Where speed is concerned, the picture is reversed: A dot matrix printer in drafting mode might well print at 350 cps plus. And even in NLQ mode, speeds of 80 cps are quite common.

■ If and when you do decide to use another printer with your PCW, you need to remember some key points. You will realise that the PCW has to be instructed to stop using its own printer and to use the other one instead. But there is more to it than that – as you will see on the next couple of pages.

Before the PCW can carry out your instruction to use another printer it has to "know" certain things:

Which printer — and how it works There is no all-embracing standard which governs how printers interpret instructions from a computer. Also, different printers have different features — for example, some matrix printers have an NLQ mode, others don't. So the PCW has to have a record of the printer's name and the list of instructions it can understand and implement. These details about the printer are held in a **printer driver** file. The PCW9512 with LOCOSCRIPT 2 comes with a range of printer drivers as standard. You can — and may have to — add others.

Which print wheel — for a daisy wheel printer Earlier on in this section I said that a daisy wheel printer prints by "moving the appropriate petal into the right position and then striking the back of the petal with a print hammer". If you think about it you will see that it can only do that if it "knows" HOW MANY petals there are on the print wheel. It also needs to know WHICH characters are on the print wheel and WHERE they are located. Don't forget, it also needs to know how many characters should be printed per inch.

We have seen that the PCW needs to know certain things about the printer so it can issue the appropriate instructions. But before it can issue those instructions it also needs to know:

HOW the instructions are to be communicated The PCW "talks" to the printer by transmitting characters and control codes along a printer cable. But the PCW can send that information "down the line" in two ways: It can either send it as a steady stream of characters, **one after the other**, like a ribbon of electrical signals; or it can chop up the stream of signals into regular lengths of, say, 8 units and then transmit them **8 at a time**.

The first method is known as **serial transmission**. The second as **parallel transmission**.

Both the printer and the PCW must be set up to work in one or other of these modes — in other words they must **both** be set up to work either via a **serial interface** or via a **parallel interface**. The key point here is that the two methods of transmission are quite different — they require different types of cabling and they require different kinds of plugs, so the PCW must know which plug socket to use when it talks to the printer.

Using other printers with Locoscript 2

Printer ports

The PCW has two printer sockets (or **printer ports**): the special Amstrad port for the standard printer and a parallel port that conforms to the Centronics standard. If you want to add a serial port, you can buy one from your dealer and attach it to the PCW at the expansion port at the rear of the monitor unit.

So, to summarise. If you decide to use another printer, bear in mind the points I have raised in this section, then work with your PCW9512 User Instructions Book to set it up properly.

PART FIVE

Automatic mailshots

■ SECTION 41
The when and why of mailshots

If you ever need to produce several copies of the same document, each one only slightly different from the others, then this Part is aimed directly at you.

So, if you are:

■ The treasurer of a club or society who has to send letters to all the members, reminding them that their subscriptions are due;

■ The chairman of a fund-raising project who has a long list of people to contact;

■ The person responsible for sending out a firm's invoices and statements;

■ The person responsible for sending out a firm's marketing mailshots;

■ The service manager or sales manager for a garage and you want to keep your existing customers in touch with new services or products;

then you have a problem which your PCW can help you overcome. Let's start by defining the problem.

Let us take a typical problem from the real world – the problem facing me. In outline it is as follows:

As well as the writing work I do, I also run specialist courses on subjects concerned with human communications – communication techniques, effective writing, effective verbal presentations, coaching and counselling, training design, etc. Although I run these courses for anyone, I do have to target a particular market sector, to make my promotional activities effective and efficient. The market sector I have chosen to target is organisations who provide financial services.

So the problem I have is to make "cold" contact with people who are already bombarded with a steady flow of "junk mail", who are not impressed easily, who expect a very personalised service, who expect a very high standard of quality in any materials which cross their desks. Put against this the fact that my "sales" message has to be somewhat nebulous, that I don't know the people concerned *and* that I don't have a very big budget and you begin to see the problem.

How can I use the PCW to help me solve the problem?

■ SECTION 41
The when and why of mailshots

Defining the problem

The first thing is that I can't afford the time or the money to visit every prospect, so an introductory letter seems to be my best vehicle for making contact. Now all those letters are going to be very similar, so one device might be to have several copies of a standard letter printed. To make it worthwhile, I would need to have at least 100 copies, but I don't need 100 copies − and in any case, how would ! personalise them ? There are bound to be small but noticeable details which will give the game away − the absence of a date for example. (Incidentally, if you look at the back of a letter which you suspect has been mass printed, you can tell. On a personally printed letter the punctuation marks create an embossed effect on the reverse of the page. If that is missing, it is a fair bet that the letter has been printed!)

My ideal solution is to print each letter individually on the PCW's printer − the quality of print is certainly good enough. But I don't want to print the same, or very nearly the same, letter over and over again. Now, one simple solution might be to create a standard letter and then edit and print each letter individually, using the original as a master. But that is a fairly time-consuming process.

What I need is some device which will enable me to slot the "personalising" information into a standard letter (either by hand, or automatically) *during* the printing process. Well I have such a device the PCW9512 with LocoScript 2!

LocoMail and mail merging

LocoScript 2 has a feature known as **LocoMail** which does the job for you. In your User Instructions Book the job it does is referred to as **mail merging** (See session 21 on page 249). This is actually quite a good descriptive title, because the way it works is by "merging" information from two sources into a single finished document. Some other word processors call it **merge printing**.

FILL and MERGE options

You can use LocoMail in either of two ways: If you have only a few letters to process, then you can **fill** in the details manually from the keyboard; but, if you have a lot of letters to process, then you can instruct the PCW to merge the details in automatically from a separate list of personal details. So LocoMail has two "modes": **FILL** mode and **MERGE** mode.

Both modes have a common starting point – a standard or "master" document, so let us prepare one which you can use if you want to.

■ SECTION 42
Creating a master letter

1 Switch your machine on and start up with a copy of your LOCOSCRIPT 2 master disk. Wait until the PCW displays the disk management screen.

2 Move your groups cursor onto the "group 1" group on drive M:

3 Tap the letter **[C]** to create a new document. Key in the name **MASTER** and then tap the **[–]** (CLEAR) key to get rid of the rest of the file name. Then tap **[ENTER]** to open the file.

■ Our *master* letter is going to be just like any other letter, except that it will have specially marked pigeon-holes set aside for the personal details we want to include later. So:

1 The first thing to do **for this exercise** is to instruct the PCW to display the text control codes, so hold down a **[SHIFT]** key and tap the **[f8/f7]** key, then tap the **[+]** (SET) key followed by the **[ENTER]** key.

2 Now, key in your own address (unless you intend to use a pre-printed letterhead).

3 Tap **[RETURN]** a couple of times to separate your address from the rest of the text.

■ We will put our first pigeon-hole in here: for the date. Now, when the PCW comes to process this letter it will print your address, then it will move the paper up a couple of lines and then it will reach the pigeon-hole which we will create in a few moments. As I said, this one is for the date, which might be one of the things which will vary from letter to letter. But how will the PCW know what to put in here? Well it can either ask YOU to supply the details, or it can look in another file on the disk. First things first, let us see how you would get the PCW to prompt you to enter the right details for this part of the letter.

■ SECTION 42
Creating a master letter

1 Tap the [+] key followed by the letter **[M]** (for "mail") and watch the screen. You can see that you have marked the start of the pigeon-hole.

2 Tell the PCW to prompt you for the details by keying in a question mark, followed by a semi-colon **[?] [;]**, followed by the words you want it to use, for example **[today's date please]** (there's no reason why we shouldn't be polite).

3 Now tap [−] (CLEAR) followed by **[M]** to mark the end of our first pigeon-hole. Then tap **[RETURN]** three times to separate the date from the next bit of the text.

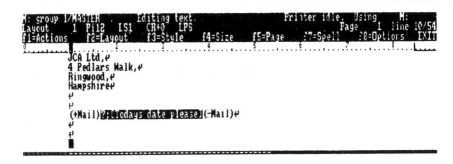

4 The next thing we want here is the name of the person we are writing to. Again this will vary from letter to letter (in other words, it is one of the **variables** as the jargon has it). So key in [+] **[M] [?] [;]** followed by **[name please]**, which in turn is followed by [−] **[M] [RETURN]**.

5 Now for the address. This is variable in more ways than one. Yes it will change from letter to letter, but more than that, there is no standard form of address − some may be just a couple of lines long (a local one for example), others may be several lines long (e.g. an international one). But LocoMail has thought of that. All you have to do is to put in a single pigeon-hole and the PCW will sort things out automatically.

Creating a master letter

■ When LocoMail comes to process this letter it will prompt you to key in details (as we have seen), but it will not process the details until you press the **[ENTER]** key. Notice that: the **[ENTER]** key.

If you key in an address in response to a LocoMail prompt, the carriage returns are processed as carriage returns and nothing else. This is a very neat solution, because with other word processors you often have to have a separate prompt for each line of the address. With LocoMail nothing is processed until you press **[ENTER]**, so it doesn't matter how many lines there are in your addresses.

6 Create the address pigeon-hole by keying in: **[+] [M] [?] [;]** **[address please] [−] [M]** then press **[RETURN]** four times, to separate the end of the address from the rest of the text (NOT to leave room for the address!!)

■ Now our next variable will be the salutation. You could use a constant like "Dear Sir" or "Sirs", but that is not very personal. On the other hand, there will be some people who you would address by name or nickname (Dear Smelly). Being slightly more formal, you may want to address someone as Mr, or Miss, or Mrs, or even Ms. (I don't know how old Smelly would react to the last three, but still...). You might even want to address someone as "Your Highness" (Smelly would definitely object to that !). The point is that it is best to treat the salutation as a variable.

7 Key in: **[+] [M] [?] [;] [salutation] [−] [M]** then tap **[RETURN]** twice and we are ready to key in the body of the letter. Key this in:

■ SECTION 42
Creating a master letter

```
M: group 1/MASTER       Editing text.           Printer idle, Using    M:
Layout    1  File   LS1  CR+0  LP6                        Page    1  line 22/54
f1=Actions   f2=Layout   f3=Style   f4=Size   f5=Page   f7=Spell   f8=Options   EXIT
.................:.........:.........:.........:.........:.........:.........L.........
JCA Ltd,⏎
4 Pedlars Walk,⏎
Ringwood,⏎
Hampshire⏎
⏎
⏎
(+Mail)█[todays date please](-Mail)⏎
⏎
⏎
(+Mail)█[Name please](-Mail)⏎
(+Mail)█[Address please](-Mail)⏎
(+Mail)█[salutation](-Mail)⏎
⏎
Having checked our records, I find that certain payments from you are
overdue. The total amount outstanding is (+Mail)█[amount](-Mail) and I would be grate
if you would send me a cheque within the next seven days.⏎
⏎
If I do not receive your payment within seven days, I shall be forced to
(+Mail)█[action to be taken](-Mail).⏎
⏎
(+Mail)█[close](-Mail)⏎
█
```

Having checked our records, I find that certain payments
from you are overdue. The total amount outstanding is [+]
[M] [?] [;] [amount] [-] [M] and I would be grateful if you
would send me a cheque within the next seven days.
[RETURN]
[RETURN]
If I do not receive your payment within seven days, I shall
be forced to [+] [M] [?] [;] [action to be taken] [−]
[M].[RETURN]
[RETURN]
[+] [M] [?] [;] [close] [-] [M] [RETURN]

8 Now save the file. Tap [EXIT] and then move the highlighting bar down to "Save and Continue" before tapping
[ENTER].

■ Notice some things about this text. Firstly, you can "drop-in" a
pigeon-hole wherever you want to include information that is
likely to vary from letter to letter (the variable does not have to
be on a line of its own).

Creating a master letter

■ Secondly, we started the letter with a variable for the salutation so we have to finish with a variable for the close (Yours sincerely, Yours faithfully, **Bye for now** and so on). Thirdly, you have allowed yourself the flexibility to treat different customers in different ways — more accurately, you have left yourself room to be as threatening or as humble as you like — it all depends on what you key in against the "action to be taken" prompt.

So, there you have your Master letter. Let us move on now to PRINT it.

1 Tap **[EXIT] [A]** and **[ENTER]** to abandon this letter (remember, you have already saved it).

2 If you intend to take a break now, BEFORE switching your machine off make a permanent copy of the MASTER letter on one of your disks. (See Section 4.)

■ **SECTION 43**
Printing a master letter (FILL)

1 With the disk Management display on screen, make sure that the files cursor is on the file called "MASTER" **not** MASTER.EG. (If you do not have a copy of this file, please work through the previous section).

Note Remember that LocoMail has two modes – FILL, in which you key in details as they are required, and MERGE, in which LocoMail reads the details in from another file and merges them with the master. Whichever mode you use, you must start by selecting the master document – the one you want to print. We will use FILL mode for our master, so:

2 Tap the letter **[F]** and then tap **[ENTER]**.

■ You will see the letter appear on screen with the cursor flashing just after the first (date) pigeon-hole.

3 Key in today's date and then tap **[ENTER]** (**[ENTER]** not repeat NOT **[RETURN]**).

■ You will see your input accepted and then the cursor moves down to the next pigeon-hole.

4 Make up some details and fill in all the pigeon-holes. **REMEMBER** press **[ENTER]** to complete an entry.

5 When you get a flag menu on screen, put some paper in the printer. Now, move the highlighting bar onto the "Print result" option and tap **[ENTER]**.

■ Because you have adjusted the printer you will see PCW9512 flashing at the top left of your screen.

6 Tap **[EXIT]** to clear the printer message, then after a short pause, tell the PCW to proceed by tapping **[ENTER]**.

■ The printer prints your "FILLED" letter and you are offered the opportunity to "Fill again" or "Finish". If you want to print another copy of this letter with some different details, by all means do so. When you have finished.

7 Move the highlighting bar down to the "Finish" option and tap **[ENTER]** to get back to the disk management screen.

The master (MERGE) document

1 Switch your machine on and start up with a copy of your LOCOSCRIPT 2 master disk. Wait until the PCW displays the disk management screen.

2 Move your files cursor onto the file called **"LETTER.2"** in the "group 1" group on the disk in A: and then tap **[E]** **[ENTER]** to "edit" this file.

NOTE The text in this section assumes that you have read the previous sections in this chapter. That being so, you will recognise where the pigeon-holes are in this letter. But you'll also recognise that they are different from the ones you have seen so far.

The first two (name and address) do not contain the prompt codes **(?;)** because this letter has been set up to be used as a MERGE document which gets the details for the pigeon-holes from another file (a data file), so it doesn't need to prompt anyone to key in anything for these slots. However, should you use this document while you are in *fill* mode, LocoMail *will* prompt you to key in details, by highlighting the name of the pigeon-hole (in capital letters, followed by a question mark).

But the third pigeon-hole is different again.

The "date" is the date on which the letter is being sent and that sort of information will not be in the data file, so here we have a special kind of **FILL** command.

For the first letter you **MERGE** print, the command works just like the fill commands you have seen and you will be prompted to key in today's date. When you do so, LocoMail fills in the pigeon-hole BUT it also makes a note of what you keyed in and stores it under the name "Date" as a **temporary variable**. For subsequent copies of the letter, LocoMail will *not* prompt you to fill in the date. Instead, the exclamation mark (!) and the word **"Date"** tell it to use whatever details it has stored under the name "Date" — which is, of course, what you keyed in for the first copy (or "PASS") of the letter. The interesting thing to note about this feature is that once LocoMail has made a note of the variable information held under the name "Date" (or any other name) you can use that same information elsewhere in the letter. For example, let's say you wanted today's date repeated in the first sentence of the letter, you could insert something like this: (Please note that) **as from [+]** **[M] [Date] [−] [M]** (we are opening...). When LocoMail reaches

■ SECTION 44
The master (MERGE) document

the mail command in the first line, it wil! automatically fill in the "Date" information.

This is a significant feature which we will expand upon when we look at data files.

3   Let us try **MERGE** printing this file. First of all, get back to the disk management display by keying in **[EXIT] [A]** and **[ENTER]**.

■ Notice that there is a file called ADDRESS2.LST near the top of the "group 1" column. That is the data file I want you to use in a few moments.

4   With your files cursor still on the file LETTER.2 tap the letter **[M]** to Merge print this MASTER DOCUMENT.

■ A flag menu appears, asking you to select a "merge data document" (that's the data file I pointed out).

5   Move your files cursor onto the file ADDRESS2.LST and tap **[ENTER]**.

■ The next flag menu asks you to confirm that it has the details correct for the job you want to do and it offers you the choice of either **Manual** or **Automatic processing**. (With manual processing you get the chance to by-pass or discard a set of details if you don't want to use it (just like when you completed a **FILL** process). With Automatic, LocoMail uses ALL the sets of data in the data file.

6   For this exercise, simply tap **[ENTER]** to go ahead with a Manual merge print.

■ You will see LocoMail fill in the name and address pigeon-holes with data it got from the data file and then it will prompt you to key in today's date. Key in today's date now, and then press **[ENTER]**.

The master (MERGE) document

■ LocoMail looks for more pigeon-holes, but it doesn't find any, so it displays a list of options. If you would like to see a printed version of this letter, go ahead and select the "Print result" option, then put paper in the printer and follow the screen prompts. Otherwise:

7 Simply tap the letter **[D]** followed by **[ENTER]** to discard these details and start another pass. Watch the screen and you will see LocoMail pick up the next set of details from the data file and merge them into the letter.

■ Notice that this time LocoMail does not prompt you for the date — it uses the details you keyed in for the first pass.

8 Tap **[D]** and **[ENTER]** at the end of each pass until you reach the end of the data file, at which point LocoMail will return you to the disk management screen.

■ SECTION 45
Creating a merge data file

■ The data file which LocoMail uses is a bit like a stack of cards — each card holding a complete set of information. But how does LocoMail know *where* on the card to find the bit of information it wants?

In data file jargon, the information on a single card is known as a **RECORD** (so each card holds a single record). Every record is comprised of the same *types* of information *in the same sequence*. Each of those types of information is known as a **FIELD**. So each record contains the same fields in the same order. Therefore, Locomail does not have to know what is in a field, or precisely where it appears on the card; it merely needs to know whether it is the first, or second, or third, or fourth, etc. field in the record.

This being so, it means that you have to set up the records in your data file in a precise and consistent way. Like this:

1 Switch your machine on and start up with a copy of your LOCOSCRIPT 2 master disk. Wait until the PCW displays the disk management screen.

2 First, let us have a look at an example data file. Move your files cursor onto the file called ADDRESS2.LST in the "group 1" column on drive A:

3 Tap **[E]** and **[ENTER]** to have a look at this file.

■ SECTION 45
Creating a merge data file

```
A: group 1/ADDRESS2.LS1  Editing text.          Printer idle. Using:
Main        Pi10   LS1    CR+0    LP5         o              Page   1 line 10 8
f1=Actions    f2=Layout    f3=Style    f4=Size    f5=Page    f7=Spell    f8=Options    EXIT
```

Name
Address;Country
Language

Mr J G Smith
589 New St
Wintlesham
Cheshire
CS4 8GT;
English

Mr F W Toabs
The Gables
Elvington Rd
Draftwell
Edinburgh

Dr H Quentin
; England
English

Mr D D Whetherall
;England

---

589 New St
Wintlesham
Cheshire

■ The screen display you have now illustrates the idea of each
record being on a separate "card". In fact each one is on a
separate page in the file. Let us look a little closer.

The first page (or record) in the file is the one which tells LocoMail
how the records in the rest of the file are made up. Notice three
things about the first page:

■ It defines how many fields there are in a record.

■ It defines the names of each of the fields.

■ It defines where one field ends and the next one begins.

Let me interpret for you. In this file there are FOUR fields in
each record. They are called: "Name", "Address", "Country"
and "Language".

The first field in every record is the **Name** field. The second field is
Address. Now that is easy enough for us to see because the
screen layout gives us lots of clues about where the name ends
and the address begins. But remember that the computer will not
be reading the screen layout. All it has to work with is a stream of

letters and spaces, so how does it tell them apart? For example. If you were to read this:

Mr Johnston Smythe Lane End Terrace Tillington

How would you know where the name ends and the address begins? It could be:

Mr Johnston, Smythe Lane, End Terrace, Tillington

Mr Johnston Smythe, Lane End Terrace, Tillington

Mr Johnston Smythe Lane, End Terrace, Tillington

Now in these examples the commas helped you interpret the same sequence of letters in different ways — they separated out the various components of the name and address. In principle LocoMail does the same thing, but it it is not limited to using commas as **separators**.

Notice that in the first record in the file, "Name" ends in a carriage return and "Address" ends in a semi-colon. Put another way, if you had been told to look at a record and find the details for an address, you would scan the record to find the first carriage return, then you would look for the first semi-colon. Once you had found them you would know that everything between those two points constituted the Address part of the record in question. Essentially, that is also how LocoMail selects the right information from each record. That being so, it is clear that you have to remember certain things when you are using a data file:

■ You have a wide choice of possible separators for any field, but you must be careful to choose one that does NOT appear in the field details. (For example, it would be silly to use a carriage return to mark the end of the address, because the address itself will contain carriage returns and how will LocoMail tell which is the right one?)

■ The name of a field is very specific. Remember that you select information for a variable by quoting its name in the **Mail** command. The field name you use must be exactly the same in both the data file and the Mail command.

■ You don't *have* to use every field in the data file in your master document. If your records contain 10 fields and you need only 1 for the job in hand, then that is fine. Remember LocoMail selects just the details you ask for in the Mail commands.

■ SECTION 45
Creating a merge data file

■ If, for some reason, you do not have any data for a particular field in one of your records (which frequently happens) you must still mark the field's place in the record – **even though the field is empty!** You will see an example of this in the records on screen. If you look at the third record, for Dr H Quentin, you will see that there are no details for the Address field, but the semi-colon is still there. So LocoMail can still find the right Country details and the right Language details.

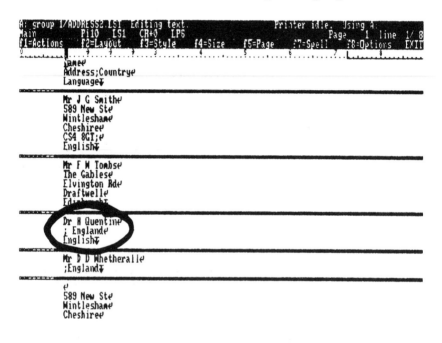

■ Earlier on we saw that when you use a special version of the FILL mail command (the "Date" example), LocoMail creates **"temporary variables"** which work just like the field names in the data file. They will remain in LocoMail's memory for the duration of a print run, but then they have to be created again, because they don't actually appear in any data file.

4 Tap **[EXIT]** then **[A]** and **[ENTER]** to abandon this file. Then move your groups cursor onto the "group 1" group on drive M:

Creating a merge data file

5 We will create our own data file. Tap **[C]** and then key in the filename **TESTDATA** and tap the **[−]** CLEAR key to delete the spare numbers followed by **[ENTER]** to open the file.

■ Before we start, we must have a clear idea of what we want to achieve and that depends on how we will be using the data in this file. So let us imagine that we are going to create a data file which we can use for mailshots to businesses. The records in our file will therefore have to hold at least the following details:

The name of the recipient
His/Her job title
The name of the company
The address of the company
The salutation
The close

Once we know this, we can go ahead and create the first record in the file − which, if you remember, defines the names and the sequence of the fields in the rest of the records in the file.

6 Key in, **[name]** and tap **[RETURN]**

■ Notice two things here; firstly, I have adopted the rule of using only lower case letters for field names to avoid confusion; secondly, I have used a carriage return to mark the end of this field, because a name field should never have to contain a carriage return. The same goes for the next two fields, so:

7 Key in **[job]** **[RETURN]** then **[company]** **[RETURN]**. Next, key in **[address]** BUT this time we cannot use a carriage return to mark the end, so tap **[;]** then without tapping the **[SPACEBAR]**, key in **[salutation]** and tap **[RETURN]** (because the salutation should never have a carriage return in it either).

8 Now key in **[close]**, but nothing else for the time being.

■ SECTION 45
Creating a merge data file

■ The close will be the last record in the field, so we need to mark the end of the record *and* the end of the page (or card, or record). The easiest way to to that is to put in a **forced** page break.

■ Hold down the **[ALT]** key and tap the **[RETURN]** key and you will see page 2 open up. You are now set up to start keying in personalised details.

Note for U.K. users: If you do decide to keep information of this sort on your computer — you *may* have to record that fact on the **Data Protection Register**. Information held for certain uses is exempt (e.g. personal, or household, or recreational uses) but it is safer to check. Contact:

> **The Office of the Data Protection Registrar**
> **Springfield House**
> **Water Lane**
> **WILMSLOW**
> **Cheshire SK5 5AX**

Let us create our first record (with imaginary details. Honestly they are imaginary, Reg'!)

10 Key in the entry you will see on the next page. Make sure you use exactly the same keystrokes.

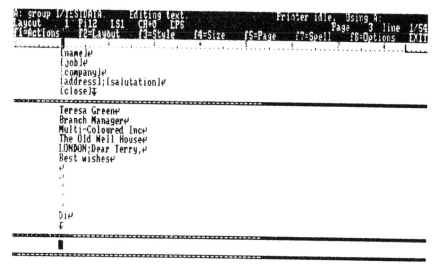

Creating a merge data file

11 Key in:

Teresa Green**[RETURN]**
Branch Manager**[RETURN]**
Multi-Coloured Inc**[RETURN]**
The Old Well House**[RETURN]**
LONDON WC1[;]Dear Terry,**[RETURN]**
Best wishes**[RETURN]**
[RETURN]
[RETURN]
[RETURN]
[RETURN]
[RETURN]
Di**[RETURN]**
[ALT][RETURN]

■ Notice that this does conform with the definition on the first page of the file. In particular, the "close" begins after the first carriage return after the semi-colon and ends with a forced page break, so all the **[RETURN]**s in the close won't confuse LocoMail.

■ Subject to the "Health Warning" above, you are now ready to create your own data file. Remember to save a permanent copy of the file though, because at the moment you are working with the memory drive.

Implementing a mailshot run

In·this final Section of this Part I want to round things off by drawing together a summary of the main points. This will take the form of a procedural checklist which sets out to answer the question: "How do I actually set about doing a mailshot run?" Of course, I can't actually answer that question, because I don't know how *you* would want to set about it. But what I *can* do is to describe how I do it, in the hope that you might pick up some ideas.

1 Start by thinking through what you want to *achieve* by doing a mailshot. Ask yourself if there is a better way of achieving the objective. **Define the problem**! In other words, check that you really do want to do a mailshot, rather than something else (like using the telephone for example).

2 You will have a mental note of the people you will be writing to. Choose one of the people from the list and write the master letter to *that person!* Forget about the others for the time being.

■ There are two reasons for writing to a specific person: Firstly, it is much easier to write the actual words if you have a clear idea of who you are "talking" to. (As an aside, while I have been writing this book I have been picturing myself explaining things to a particular friend who is quite intelligent, but who knows little if anything about word processors). Secondly, you will arrive at a more natural layout for the letter.

3 Once you have saved a copy of the letter, get a print out of it and then go through the text marking up those items which will vary from copy to copy. Also check that the letter is appropriate for everyone you will be writing to.

4 Edit the letter, replacing the variable items with "Mail" commands.

■ If you intend to FILL this letter and you think you will need prompts, use the form of the Mail command which includes the "? ;" prompt definitions.

Implementing a mailshot run

5 Save the edited version of the master letter. If you are going to FILL the letter you are now ready to test if it works as you intended.

6 If you are going to MERGE print the letter, you will next need to create your data file.

■ If you already have a data file, you will need to check that the records in the file contain the information you will need for your letter and you must make sure that the letter and the data file both use the same names for the variables (e.g. if you have marked a pigeon-hole in your letter as being the slot for the "salutation", check that you haven't called it something else, such as the "start", in the data file).

7 Define how you are going to use the data file (not *just* for the job in hand – think also about any follow-up there may be to this mailshot).

8 Create the data file as we discussed earlier in this section. **REMEMBER**, that if you do not have data for one of the fields, you must still mark its position. In other words, even if a field is empty it *must* still appear in the record once you have defined that it will.

9 Carry out a test MERGE print run.

10 If all is OK, go ahead with the real print run.

PART SIX

Care and maintenance skills

■ SECTION 47
Introduction

You can do most of your **housekeeping** jobs while you have Locoscript running. But from time to time you may want to work on a number of disks and files and do several housekeeping jobs in one session. When this happens, you will find it much quicker to do the jobs *without* starting up Locoscript first.

This Part describes how to do these jobs with your CP/M operating system. Very briefly, you work with CP/M when you want to use the PCW as a general-purpose computer.

■ SECTION 48
Looking after your disks

The following points should *always* be borne in mind:

■ You must beware of damaging your disks, because if you do, it is almost certain that you will lose all the files on the disk. SO **always** have at least two copies of every disk: the *master and the back-up* (which is simply a duplicate copy of the master). This may sound a bit over the top, but what costs more – a disk, or the time you would have to spend re-creating it?

■ Make back-ups of program disks as soon as you get them. IF YOU HAVE NOT MADE COPIES OF THE PCW's MASTER DISKS, DO SO NOW! (See Section 4.)

■ Once you start working with your PCW you will start to create document files. You should back-up those files, at the end of each working session at the very least.

■ If, during a working session, you create or edit several files, then you should back-up each file as soon as you finish working with it.

■ **Always** store master disks and back-ups in separate boxes and, preferably, in separate rooms.

■ **Always** store disks in a dust-proof container of some kind.

■ **Always** store disks at normal room temperatures.

■ **Never** touch the magnetic surfaces of the disk (which is, after all only a flimsy sheet of plastic coated with a magnetic medium). The rigid casing gives the impression that a disk is unbreakable – don't be fooled!

■ **Never** allow the disks to get close to a stray magnetic field, e.g. an electric motor or a buzzer.

■ **Never** switch your computer ON or OFF when you have a disk in a drive.

■ As a general rule, try to keep data files (the work you've done) on separate disks from programs (program files).

■ Make sure that you establish a routine procedure for indentifying disks (and what's on them). For example, keep word processing document files on one disk and spreadsheet data files on another.

Resetting (rebooting) the PCW

You will probably be using the PCW mostly for word processing. But what happens if you decide to use the PCW for something other than word processing? Or you want to reorganise your filing system? It is true that you can do many of the typical housekeeping tasks via the word-processing system, but is there a quicker way? Well, yes there is. Let's assume that your machine is already switched on.

1 Start by getting your working copy of the CP/M Plus disk and put it in the disk drive (the left-hand one if you have two disk drive slots).

2 With your left hand, hold down the keys labelled **[SHIFT]** and **[EXTRA]**, then with your right hand, tap the key labelled **[EXIT]**. You will see the PCW go through its CP/M start-up sequence.

3 Holding down **[SHIFT]** and **[EXTRA]**, then tapping the **[EXIT]** key is the procedure you use to **reset**, or **reboot** (yes honestly), your computer. If you don't know what that means, have a look in the *Glossary*.

The RESET procedure overrides anything the computer is doing at the time, **but be careful with it**, because resetting the PCW involves flushing out the memory and the memory drive (drive M). So if you had been working on something and you had not saved it on disk, you would lose it forever. Also, with certain software packages, you might scramble the data files if you do not close down properly **before** resetting!

If you reset the computer with the Locoscript disk in the drive, then you will simply re-start Locoscript. But if you reset with the CP/M Plus disk in the drive, you will get access to the CP/M Plus operating sytem.

You will know when the operating system has loaded, because several lines of text will appear on screen and then the disk light will go out. On the last of the lines of text to appear you will see:

A>

This the known as the **A prompt** or CP/M's **system prompt**. It lets you know that CP/M is ready to carry out your instructions.

■ SECTION 50
Naming and storing your document files

When you create a document file (or any other kind of file) which you intend to store on a disk, you will have to give it a name. That name will have to conform with the following simple rules:

■ **Two parts** The file names you use can have two parts: a *title* and an *extension*, or type code, to identify what type of file it is, e.g. a letter, a report, a quotation and so on. You don't *have* to use both parts, but if you do, you must separate them with a full point, e.g.

thispage.txt
bankman.let
brown.qut

■ **Title part** can be anything betweeen one and eight characters in length.
■ **Extension part** can be anything between one and three characters in length.

You **must not** have a space anywhere in your file name and you **must not** use a full stop other than to separate the title and the extension. If you need to split the file title into more than one part for, say, the chapters of a book, use the hyphen symbol, e.g. **pcw-6.txt.**

You can use most of the keys on the keyboard in your file names, but for day-to-day purposes I would advise you to stick to letters and numbers. You won't make any mistakes that way, but perhaps more importantly, you're more likely to be able to interpret your file names in six months' time. After all, you store a file so you can refer to it at some time in the future and that means you must be able to find the file again. So keep your file names simple! Use a system that comes naturally to you, or one that fits in with the way you do thinks normally.

It doesn't matter whether you key in the file name in capitals or in lower case. The computer will convert all letters into capitals.

Caution Certain file extensions have specific meanings to your computer and some have specific meanings to particular software packages, so be careful with them. In particular, **do not use** COM, EXE, HEX, ASM, BAS, PRN, INT, SUB or $$$ unless you are told to in the instructions for the software you are using at the time.

■ SECTION 51
Finding out what is on a disk

When you start up your word-processing system in the normal way, the screen displays a complete list of the files on your disk — separated into groups. If you change the disk in the drive and then tap the [f1] key that display will change to tell you which files and groups are on the new disk. So when you are word processing it is very easy, but perhaps a bit cumbersome to find what you are looking for.

But what happens if you decide to use the PCW for something other than word processing? Or if you just want to keep your filing system up to date? Or if you have simply lost track of a file you need? Is there a quicker way to get a listing of the files on a disk? Well, yes there is. Let's assume that your machine is already switched on.

1 Start by getting your working copy of the disk labelled "CP/M Plus" and put it in the disk drive (the left hand one if you have two disk drive slots).

2 With your left hand, hold down the keys labelled [SHIFT] and [EXTRA], then with your right hand, tap the key labelled [EXIT]. You will see the PCW go through its CP/M start up sequence.

3 Holding down [SHIFT] and [EXTRA], then tapping the [EXIT] key is the procedure you use to "RESET", or "REBOOT" your computer. If you don't know what that means, put a place marker on this page and have a look in the *glossary*. Or, if you want to know more about the topic, read the pages near the start of this chapter headed: "RESETTING (REBOOTING) THE PCW".

4 When you reset with the CP/M Plus disk in the drive, and when you get the "A>" prompt on screen, CP/M is ready to accept your commands.

■ SECTION 51

Finding out what is on a disk

5 We want to get a list or "directory" of the files on a disk, but if you enter the directory command now, you will get a list of the files on the CP/M disk — not the one you want to check out. So replace the CP/M disk with the one you want to check and THEN key in: **DIR** and press the **[RETURN]** or **[ENTER]** key. You will see a list of the file names appear on screen.

```
CP/M Plus  Amstrad Consumer Electronics plc

v 1.4, 61K TPA, 1 disc drive, 112K drive M:

A>dir
A: J14CPM3   EMS : PROFILE  ENG : RPED     BAS : RPED     SUB : BASIC    COM
A: DIR       COM : DISCKIT  COM : ED       COM : ERASE    COM : LANGUAGE COM
A: PALETTE   COM : PAPER    COM : PIP      COM : RENAME   COM : SET      COM
A: SET24X80  COM : SETDEF   COM : SETKEYS  COM : SETLST   COM : SETSIO   COM
A: SHOW      COM : SUBMIT   COM : TYPE     COM : KEYS     WP
A>█
```

NOTE that you were given a directory of the disk in drive A: (you can tell that because each line of filenames is preceded by "A:") There are three things to notice here and we examine them on the next page:

■ When you start up under CP/M, the computer assumes (in default of any contrary instruction from you) that any command you key in applies to the disk in drive A: (in other words, drive A: is its "default drive") And that's why you got a **DIR**ectory of the disk in drive A:

■ You can elect to work on another drive, by simply keying in the identifying letter of the drive you want and then pressing [RETURN] e.g. **M: [RTN]** or **m: [RTN]**.This process is known as "logging-on" to a drive.

■ You can get a directory for another disk drive without having to log-on to that drive. For example, if you now want to find out which files are in the memory drive (drive M:), but you don't want to log to that drive, key-in:

DIR M: [RTN]

Twin drive machines

If you have a twin drive machine, put a disk in the right hand drive now!

■ SECTION 51
Finding out what is on a disk

Try keying in: **DIR B**:

You will get a list of the files on the disk in drive B.

Single drive machines

On a single drive machine, when you ask for a directory of drive B: you hit a slight logical problem: you have only one drive – and that's called drive A:! But the PCW can cope. The screen prompts you to provide a disk for B:

What it means is: "For the time being, let's pretend that your drive A: is called drive B:, so put another disk in the drive then tap the **[SPACEBAR]** to let me know when you've done it." (Clever isn't it!?)

6 Now, normally, you would do as you are told. But let us cheat a bit. *don't* change the disk. Just tap the **[SPACEBAR]**. And away goes the PCW, giving you a directory of what it thinks is drive B: again, you can tell because each row of filenames is now preceded by "B:" (so it's not so clever after all!)

The **DIR** command has other variants which you might find useful, so it is worth looking in the PCW User Instruction Manual.

■ SECTION 52
Matching up file names (masks)

There will be times when you want to carry out the same command for several files with very similar names (for example, make a copy of a set of files called CHAP1, CHAP2, CHAP3, etc.). There will also be times when you are looking for a file who's name you cannot remember exactly. CP/M has a feature which you will find useful under these and many other circumstances. CP/M allows you to use **AMBIGUOUS FILE NAMES** in many of your commands.

You create an ambiguous file name by replacing parts of the name with special symbols. You can use the question mark symbol (?) to represent a single character, or you can use the asterisk (*) symbol to represent a group of characters. E.g.

■ To make a copy on drive M: of several files with similar names (which are on the disk in drive A:) you would key in:

PIP M:=A:CHAPTER? [RTN]

In response to this **single** command, CP/M will copy **all** the files which match the ambiguous name. (See also *"Making a duplicate copy of a document file"*)

■ To find a file called "LETTER.(something-or-other)", key in:

DIR LETTER.* [RTN]

In the first example you could have used **CHAP*** as your ambiguous filename. In the second example you could have used **LETTER???**. Just remember that a question mark takes the place of a single character and the asterisk represents several characters. So:

■ ????????.??? and *.* means all files called "something dot something". In other words: **all files!** So the command: DIR followed by either of these two and then [RTN] will give you a normal directory: (e.g. DIR *.* [RTN]).

■ ???????? or * on its own means all files which do not have a file TYPE extension. (e.g: DIR???????? [RTN]).

■ ????.* means any file which has only four characters in the first name and has any file type extension.

■ *.? means a file which has any name, but which has only one character in its file type extension. There are many more possible combinations for you to try.

■ SECTION 53

Checking the space left on a disk

You can get a lot of information on a disk, but there is a limit. Before you start what looks like being a lengthy job, it is a good idea to check that there will be enough room on the disk for the document you are going to create. The precise amount you need will vary with the page layout, but for word processing, if you work on a maximum of 65 characters per line, with 55 lines per page (for 11 inch continuous paper), you can see that you will have to allow for roughly 65*55 or 3575 characters for each page. (In practice, an average of 2.5 to 3 thousand characters per page is usually close enough). So now you know how much space you need, how do you find out how much you've got?

Well you need the CP/M program called **SHOW.COM** which is on your CP/M disk. So make sure you have your working copy of the disk to hand.

1 Put your working copy of the CP/M disk in drive A: (**If you have two drive slots** the left hand one is drive A: also put any other disk in the right-hand drive).

2 RESET your system — Hold down **[SHIFT]** and **[EXTRA]**. Then tap the **[EXIT]** key. The PCW will carry out a series of jobs (e.g. reading certain files on the disk in A: and putting copies of them onto the memory drive — drive M:).

3 When the PCW screen settles down and you get the system prompt (A>) key in: **SHOW B: [RTN]** With a twin drive system, the PCW goes ahead, but with the single drive system you'll be prompted to provide a disk for B: first. For now, just tap the **[SPACEBAR]** as if you had swapped disks.

4 The SHOW command tells the PCW to look at the disk in the drive you have specified (B: in this case) and report on how much free space remains. You should see a display something like this:

B: RW, Space 100k

5 The "RW" signifies that you can "read" from this disk and "write" to it — i.e. use it normally.

■ SECTION 53

Checking the space left on a disk

6 "Space 100k" tells you that you have enough room to fit another 100 thousand ("100k") "bytes" on the disk. (Think of a "byte" as one character – see also the Glossary.)

■ SECTION 54
Making a duplicate copy of a document file

When you want to tidy-up or reorganise your disk filing system, one of the jobs you will want to do is to make copies of one or more files. (Don't forget that you will also need to make safety (back-up) copies of all your files – see Section 47.)

So how do you make copies of a *file* rather than a disk? Well you need the CP/M program called PIP.COM which is on your CP/M disk. So make sure you have your working copy of the disk to hand. (Incidentally, the PIP program has several other uses, see your instructions book).

1 Put your working copy of the CP/M disk in drive A: (**If you have two drive slots** the left hand one is drive A:).

2 RESET your system – Hold down [**SHIFT**] and [**EXTRA**]. Then tap the [**EXIT**] key. The PCW will carry out a series of jobs. (One of those jobs is to read certain files on the disk in A: (**INCLUDING PIP.COM**) and put copies of them onto the memory drive (drive M:). This is PIP.COM in action, under the control of the PCW. As you can see, it can even copy itself!

3 When the PCW screen settles down and you get the system prompt (A>) key in: **M:** [**RTN**] You will see the "system prompt" change to (**M>**) which tells you that M: is now your default drive (see the Glossary). (If you key in: **DIR [RTN]** you wil see which files are on the M: drive).

4 Leave your CP/M disk in drive A: for the time being, but let's pretend for the moment that it is one of your "data" disks which holds files you want to copy. (REMEMBER, that we are "logged" to the M: drive and there is a copy of PIP.COM on this drive).

5 Let us further suppose that you want to make a duplicate copy of a file you have called "SHOW.COM" and you want that copy on M: (In reality of course you would not use the "COM" extension – see Section 49).

6 Key in: **PIP M:SHOW.COM=A:SHOW.COM** (DON'T press [RTN] yet).

Turn to the next page for a breakdown of this command!

■ SECTION 54

Making a duplicate copy of a document file

- Remember, you want to use **PIP.COM** (the copying program) so that is the first thing you key in, but, because it is a **COM**mand program you don't need to key in the full name **to RUN the program**.

- Notice also that the PIP command is separated from the rest of the instruction by a space *and* that there are no other spaces in the instruction. PIP is the command the other details are known as **"PARAMETERS"** to the command.

- Notice how the parameters are expressed. They are in the form of a mathematical equation which describes *how you want things to be* — rather than what you want PIP to *do*! You want to end up with a file on M: called SHOW.COM (M:SHOW.COM to be precise) which is going to be the same as (or equal to) a file on A: called SHOW.COM.

7   If that's clear, press [RTN] now to implement the PIP command. If it's not, turn to Section 56.

■ SECTION 55
Getting rid of unwanted files

From time to time you will want to clear old files from your disks
– to make more room, or simply to minimise the clutter. Here's
how you do it.

1   Start by double checking that you really do not need to
keep the file. If you *do* need the file, but you don't want it
on the disk you are using, you can COPY the file onto
another disk (see Section 53).

■ The structure of the command to use is:

ERA file-name [RTN]

2   So to **ERA**se a file called LETTER.TXT which is on the drive
you are "logged" to, you would key in:
ERA LETTER.TXT [RTN]

3   To **ERA**se a file which is on a drive OTHER THAN the one
you are logged to, you must precede the file-name with
the appropriate drive identifier. E.g:

ERA B:LETTER.TXT [RTN]

4   To **ERA**se a group of files with similar names you can use
file name masks – see Section 51
ERA B:LETTER.* [RTN]

Note: The PCW will check that you really do want to erase a
number of files. You will have to confirm by tapping the letter [Y].
You can erase several, or even *all*, the files on a disk in one go by
using file name masks. As an added safety measure you can get
the PCW to check with you before it erases each file (provided you
have a copy of ERASE.COM available preferably on the disk you
are logged to). So, assuming you were logged to drive M: – with
ERASE.COM on that drive (i.e. copied across from the CP/M disk),
you can selectively erase all the files on the disk in drive A: with
this command:

ERA A:*.* [C] then press the **RETURN** key

The PCW will present you with the name of a file on the disk and
then ask you to *confirm* that you do want it erased, before
removing the file from the disk.

■ SECTION 55
Getting rid of unwanted files

NOTE: The ERAse command does NOT put the file into "limbo" as Locoscript's erase/delete procedure does. Once you have ERAsed a file you cannot get it back — unless you have special software.

■ SECTION 56
Renaming a document file

From time to time you will want to give your files different names (e.g. because you have changed your filing system, or more often because you want to denote that a file is a "back-up" copy of another file). This is how you do it:

1 To rename a file which is called LETTER.TXT and to give it the new name LETTER.BAK you would key in:

REN LETTER.BAK=LETTER.TXT [RTN]

Note the formula: NEWNAME = OLDNAME!!!

2 If you want to change the name of a file which is on a disk OTHER THAN the one you are working on (i.e. other than the one you are "logged to") you will have to precede the file names with the appropriate drive identifying letter. For example, if you are logged to drive M: and you want to change the name of a file which is on drive A: you would key in:

REN A:LETTER.BAK=A:LETTER.TXT [RTN]

NOTE: The REName command changes only the name of the file — it does not affect the file in any other way.

■ SECTION 57

Some general points about CP/M commands

A "typical" CP/M command takes the following form:

PIP M:SHOW.COM=A:SHOW.COM [RTN]

We are using PIP in this example, but the points I am going to make here apply generally to CP/M commands.

1 A copy of the program must be on the disk in the drive which you have logged to. If you are logged to drive A: and PIP.COM is on drive M: then you would have to precede the command with the drive "identifier", i.e. you would have to key in **M:PIP**, etc.

2 You write the command line in the form of an equation. Here, it reads: "make a copy so we end up with a file on M: called SHOW.COM. which is the same as the file on A: called SHOW.COM". Think of CP/M commands as having the form "**destination = source**".

3 If you want the copy to have the same name as the original file, there is no need to specify the name for the "destination" file, e.g.

PIP M:=A:SHOW.COM [RTN]

would be OK.

4 If you want the copy to have a different name from the original, then you have to specify that name (for the destination file) in the command: e.g.

PIP M:LETTER.BAK=A:LETTER.TXT [RTN]

would create a file called LETTER.BAK on M: which is a copy of the file LETTER.TXT on the disk in your drive A:

5 You can use file name masks in many CP/M commands. For example, let's imagine we want to copy ALL the "COM" files on a disk into memory. You would key in:

PIP M:=A:*.COM [RTN]

To copy all files called "SHOW" something, you would key in:

PIP M:=A:SHOW.* [RTN]

■ SECTION 57

Some general points about CP/M commands

■ **To copy ALL the files onto M: key in: PIP M:=A:*.* [RTN]** (for more information see Section 51)

■ Remember that to work with a file which is on a disk other than the one you are logged to, you must identify the drive which holds the program, e.g:

A:PIP M:=A:SHOW.COM [RTN]

Glossary

ALT key A key that works like a "super" shift key. It enables the PCW keyboard to generate ALTernative results from the various keys on the keyboard.

Ambiguous file names With the CP/M operating system you can key in commands that include file names incorporating *wildcards*, i.e. characters that represent another character, thus creating a file name — *mask* — that can apply to more than one file. In this sense such file names are ambiguous.

Back-up Used as a verb, this is the process of creating duplicate copies of files or disks. Used as a noun, it signifies a duplicate — safety — copy of a file or disk.

BASIC A computer programming language used in microcomputers.

Booting The start-up procedure for a computer system, during which the computer *reads-in* the operating system from disk.

CAN key The key with which you CANcel or abandon most Locoscript activity menus. You would use it if you hit the wrong key, or if you change your mind half way through the activity.

Command An instruction (or a set of instructions) keyed in at the keyboard, telling the computer to carry out a particular job.

COM The file name extension used for a *command file* — one that holds a computer program written in the computer's internal language.

COPY key The key with which you mark the start and finish of a block of text you want to copy.

CP/M Standing for *Command Program for Microcomputers*, this is — the operating system for the PCW9512 and other 8-bit computers.

Cursor A marker on your screen, usually a bar or rectangle of light. It is there to tell you where you are working on the screen display.

Cursor keys A set of keys marked with arrows pointing up, down, left and right. You use these keys to move the cursor around the screen.

CUT key The key with which you mark text that you want to remove from a document. ("CUT text CUT" removes and discards the marked text. A combination of COPY and CUT removes it from the document on screen, but keeps a copy of the marked text in memory.)

Glossary

Data disk A disk on which you store files you have created by using a computer program – such as LocoScript 2.

Data file A file that holds information generated by a computer program. Strictly speaking, your LocoScript document files are data files. But *within* LocoScript 2, the term is used to refer to files that LocoMail will use during merge printing. In this context a data file is a store of information – a collection of records.

Default settings When you start up a program such as LocoScript 2 it has to make certain assumptions about the way you want to work. It has to adopt standard settings for a wide range of things. Thus, the program will work in a particular way in *default* of any instructions to the contrary. In other words, it will adopt certain default settings.

Delete To rub out or erase characters you have typed in by mistake. *Delete left* means deleting characters to the left of the cursor. *Delete right* means deleting the character on which the cursor is positioned (thus moving the deletion to the right through the text). You can also delete blocks (CUT) and files.

Disk A flat circular piece of plastic with a magnetic surface that you use to store permanent copies of data and program files. Disks for the PCW9512 are housed in a hard plastic shell that has slots to enable the computer to read the information stored on the disk.

Disk drive The part of the computer system that spins the disk in its protective covering while reading or writing information on its surface.

Document In LocoScript 2 terminology a document is *any* piece of text that has its own separate identity and is stored in a file of its own.

Documentation The manuals supplied with your PCW that explain how to use the hardware and software.

Dot-matrix printer A printer that uses a set of pins to create a pattern of dots on paper. By varying the pattern you create the shapes of the different characters.

Editing The process of amending, inserting or deleting text and changing document layouts.

ENTER key The key with which you *enter*, i.e. confirm, your instructions or selections from menus.

Glossary

EXIT key The key with which you terminate most LocoScript activities and modes of operation.

Field In the context of a LocoMail data file, the smallest unit of data. Each data file holds a number of *records* and each record is made up of individual *fields*.

Field name In order to use the data in the fields and records of a data file, each separate field in a record must be given a name — a *field name*.

File A collection of information stored as a separate entity with its own special file name. You can have data files and program files, i.e. files that hold programs.

File name mask *See* Ambiguous file names.

Flag menu A small temporary menu, sometimes called a *pull-down menu*, that appears on screen as and when it is required. It looks like a small flag.

Floppy disk A flexible sheet of recording material in the shape of a disk. A PCW disk does not seem to be floppy, because the shell that holds the disk itself is made of rigid plastic. *See also* Disk.

Format Used as a noun, this signifies either the layout of a page, or the method adopted for organising the storage space on a disk. Used as a verb: to prepare a disk for use on your computer system by laying down a new pattern of magnetic *tracks* on its surface ready to store information.

Function keys A set of keys on your computer keyboard with which you gain access to various LocoScript activities.

Hard copy A copy of your document file that has been printed out on paper. Also called a *printout*.

Hardware The physical components that make up your computer system, such as the keyboard, disk drive, monitor, printer.

Housekeeping Those necessary activities that are not concerned directly with using your PCW as a word processor or a computer, but without which things would soon get in a mess. For example, carrying out routine checks of what information you are holding on a particular disk, erasing unwanted material, renaming files, copying files, making backups.

Input The process of getting information into a computer system, or the information that has been put in to a computer system.

Glossary

Justification The process of lining text up to a margin. The text in this glossary is *right-justified* as well as *left-justified*.

K The abbreviation for *kilo*, or 1000, in the computer world. Your PCW has a memory capable of holding 512,000 *bytes* (or characters) of information, so it is referred to as a 512K computer. Actually there are 1024 bytes in one kilobyte, so in computer terminology 1K actually means "near enough a thousand".

Memory The computer's *internal store* in which it holds programs and data while you are working with them.

Memory drive A part of the computer's memory that has been set aside so you can work with it as if it were a disk drive. Sometimes called a *Ram drive*. This drive exists only when the computer is switched on − switching the PCW off flushes out the whole memory − so the memory drive should be regarded as a temporary storage medium.

Menu A list displayed by a computer program that tells you which activities are available at a particular point in the computer program. LocoScript has lots of menus. In fact, the menus are a major feature of its operations. Programs such as LocoScript are often said to be *menu-driven*.

Monitor A high-quality screen or *visual display unit* (VDU) that enables you to see what you are keying in, as you key it in. It also displays the results of the computer's processing activity.

Mouse A device that enables you to *input* instructions to the computer by moving a pointer on your screen (so it points at a picture or a menu), rather than keying in lengthy sequences of commands.

Operating system A type of computer program that controls, or manages, the way the computer and all the other items of hardware operate as a single system. (*See* CP/M.)

Output To transmit information from the computer (or some other device), or the information you get out of your computer (via the printer, or a disk drive, or on screen).

Overwrite To write data on top of data that is already stored in the computer's memory and thus replace it.

PASTE key The key with which you insert a block of text or a standard phrase into the text on screen, starting at the point where the cursor is positioned.

Glossary

Printer The machine attached to the computer which prints out hard copies of the work you have been doing.

Prompt An instruction on the screen telling you what to do next.

Proportional spacing of text On a typewriter and on the PCW's screen, an 'i' takes up the same amount of space as an 'm'. With proportional spacing, the different sizes of the letters are taken into account when the text is laid out, so an 'i' takes up about half the space of an 'm'.

Quit To finish doing a particular job with your software, or finish working with the software itself.

RAM (Random Access Memory) That part of the computer's memory that is available for you to use for loading and running programs, for the memory drive and for entering and processing data. When you switch off your PCW everything stored in the RAM is lost, including anything stored in the memory drive.

RAM drive *See* Memory drive.

Record A single set of data held in a data file. A data *file* contains a number of *records*, each one consisting of individual *fields*.

Reformat To change the layout, i.e. the format, of text, giving it, for example, different margins, page lengths and so on.

Reset To repeat the start-up or booting procedure.

RETURN key The key that, in LocoScript, performs the same function as a typewriter's carriage-return key. When you use the PCW under CP/M the **[RETURN]** key has the same function as the **[ENTER]** key.

ROM (Read-only Memory) The computer memory in which information is stored permanently and cannot be altered by any program instructions.

Separator In the context of a data file, a separator is a symbol of some kind that separates one field from the next — in other words it marks where one field ends and another begins.

Saving The process of storing copies of documents, data or program files on disk. For permanent storage, the files should be saved on a floppy disk — not on the memory disk drive. When you are word processing, you should save frequently, for example, after keying in each page of text.

Glossary

Scrolling The process of moving your screen display up and down or side to side to enable you to get a particular section of the display on screen ready for work.

Software Programs that enable the very stupid hardware to do a useful job of work. LocoScript is one kind of *applications software*, CP/M is a type of *systems software*.

Text The words and characters (letters, numbers, spaces and symbols) that make up a finished document.

VDU *See* Monitor.

Wildcards A character that can be used to represent another character (just like wildcards in poker). Under CP/M there are two wildcard characters, '?' and '*'. The '?' represents any other single character, the '*' represents any group of characters.

Word processor A computer driven by a software program that enables you to carry out the tasks of writing, editing and printing all kinds of documents. Sometimes also used of the word processing program itself.

Word wrap A word-processing feature in which the word processor works out where a line of text should end and it then *wraps* any uncompleted word down to the left-hand end of a new line. So you can keep typing without having to worry about when you get to the end of your typing line.

WYSIWYG A word-processing feature, pronounced 'whizzywig', in which the screen display emulates precisely how the finished document will look on the page – What You See Is What You Get!

Write-protect tab A small tab on the PCW's floppy disks that in one position allows you to read and write to the disk. When moved to another position the tab still allows the disk to be read, but it prevents the computer from writing to the disk; thus the disk is *write-protected*.

Index

Index

Index